Program Outcome Evaluation: A Step-by-Step Handbook

By Kristine L. Mika

Families International, Inc.
Milwaukee, Wisconsin

Copyright 1996
Families International, Inc.
Publishing in association with Family Service America
11700 West Lake Park Drive
Milwaukee, WI 53224

Library of Congress Cataloging-in-Publication Data

Mika, Kristine L.
    Program outcome evaluation : a step-by-step handbook / by Kristine
    L. Mika.
        p.   cm.
    Includes bibliographical references.
    ISBN 0–87304–286–7 (pbk.)
    1. Evaluation research (Social action programs)   I. Title.
HV11.5.M56 1996
    361.2'5'072—dc20   96–44909

Printed in the United States of America

Contents

Acknowledgments

I would like to thank Robert Nordstrom for giving me the opportunity to write this book and for his patience and support throughout its preparation. I am also grateful for the helpful feedback from my colleagues Miriam Kluger and Eleanor Lyon.

I would also like to thank my parents, Emil and Stella Rogalski, for their loving support and my sister, Kathy Carey, who ingeniously intervened during my writer's block with a recording of Hildegard Von Bingen's "Canticles of Ecstasy." Writing came more easily with 12th-century church music in the background.

In the past seven years two friends and teachers have given me more than their share of patience, kindness, and support. Rodney Elizabeth Dary has always been there to guide me through the good times and bad. Nicholas Anastasiow has always been my anchor in the sometimes calm but mostly wild waters of evaluation and education. He gave me the strength to continue when I didn't feel like it and the opportunity to practice my writing skills. With respect and affection I thank you both.

Finally, a big Labrador retriever hug and a couple of hot dogs for my faithful companion—Margo—that glamorous buttercup Labrador who stayed by my side, made me laugh, and retrieved me for trips to Dragon Fly Pond at just the right moments.

1

Introduction

Key Terms

Program: A design of activities that, in theory, produce an expected change among participants within a given time frame.

Program outcome effectiveness: The expected and observed change in a program participant.

Program outcome evaluation: Designed, planned activities to measure program outcome effectiveness and to compare actual results with expected results or program standards of success. A basic program outcome evaluation describes the outcome results at scheduled points in time.

Stakeholders: All persons or groups of persons who have an interest in a program's ability to meet its standards successfully.

■ Introduction

The words *program evaluation* commonly trigger a wide range of responses among program administrators, directors, and staff, especially in agencies that have not regularly evaluated the outcomes of programs. Staff seldom embrace program evaluation as a "fun project." Rather, they tend to view it in authoritarian terms. They may feel as though they personally are being watched and evaluated and often associate it with extreme changes in program structure, personnel, and even program existence. Some staff members may view program evaluation as a nuisance task that cuts into getting the "real" work of service provision done. Obviously, such reactions can subvert the effective monitoring of program outcomes and put the program at risk of that which staff fear most—program cuts, changes in staffing, and possible elimination of the program.

It does not have to be this way.

Program evaluation results, especially results tracked over time, offer funders insight into a program's success with its participants and the efforts of its staff. Programs that demonstrate in concrete terms observable change that can be measured on a regular basis prove their credibility and ability to serve participants well. Although no program, regardless of its success, is guaranteed protection from cuts, funders are more likely to cut programs that do not show any evidence of success than programs that show evidence of success, change, and growth.

The Joint Commission on Accreditation of Healthcare Organizations (1992), in its *1993 Accreditation Manual*, states that such an approach to evaluation and assessment "can interfere with [the pursuit of] lifelong self-assessment and constant personal growth" (p. 18). Simply designed evaluations that are conducted regularly offer staff *ongoing* opportunities for program review and development. Such evaluation studies provide a "snapshot" of the program within a particular time frame and offer a wealth of information on program trends and directions when these "snapshots" are reviewed over time.

Good evaluation methods and tools help program staff assess the needs and concerns of program participants and thus deliver quality services that address these needs and concerns. Evaluation results provide essential information for making decisions that affect participants as well as the life of the program.

■ Purpose of Program Outcome Evaluation

Program outcome evaluation activities measure expected changes in program participants. The results of a program outcome evaluation are used to make decisions regarding whether a program is doing what it is designed to do and whether it is doing it consistently well. Program evaluation provides critical information about the program's ongoing development and health. Results should not be feared. Rather, they should be used to provide staff and administrators with information that allows them to improve the program. Evaluation results should not collect dust in a file cabinet; they should be used to determine whether program components should be continued, revised, expanded, or eliminated by program staff.

Continuation

Whether a program should be continued as it currently operates should be based on evaluation results indicating that the program is facilitating desired changes among program participants and that no immediate or future considerations have been identified that might suggest the need for revisions. However, program areas to watch or specific groups of participants to watch may be identified. These program "alerts" might be based on slight changes in the outcome results or shifts in the types of participants in the program that over time might call for program revision or expansion.

Revision

The decision to revise a program is based on results indicating that the program has evident weaknesses and that changes are needed in order to align outcome results with outcome goals. For example, a program may need to be revised if it isn't quite meeting its standards for success despite the fact that the participants it serves and the program's operations have not changed.

Expansion

The decision to expand a program is generally based on results indicating that the population that it serves is growing or shifting and specific changes are needed to accommodate such growth or shifts in order to maintain the outcome standards. Expansion might include adding staff or developing new components to the program to accommodate new participant subgroups and/or staff training.

Elimination

The decision to eliminate a program is based on indications that the program is not achieving and cannot reach expected standards for success. The decision to eliminate a program is often difficult and is usually based on a long-term pattern of unsatisfactory results.

Programs targeted for elimination do not serve its participants. The hard evidence of program evaluation results cannot be dismissed lightly. Although program evaluation puts programs at some risk of discovering their weaknesses, the insecurity and disequilibrium that arise out of such risk are minimal compared with the waste of resources devoted to programs that do not work. Moreover, program administrators and key staff who truly understand the strengths and potential of a program can use identified weaknesses to strengthen the program if they judge that it is salvageable or to replace it with a program that works.

■ Stakeholders

Every program has several groups of stakeholders, that is, the people who have an interest in the program's success. Program evaluation results are used by a wide range of stakeholders to make various kinds of decisions that affect the program and its participants. Stakeholder groups include the following:

- *Staff* seeking feedback on their combined efforts as well as on the combined impact they have had in serving program participants.
- *Funders and administrators* seeking confirmation that their money is well spent and that future budget requests are justified.
- *Participants and potential participants* seeking programs that actually do what they say they are doing for program participants.
- *Potential staff* who wish to work in creative environments that nurture them professionally.
- *Other programs or organizations* seeking to collaborate with a program.
- *Community network and referral agencies* that wish to refer community members to the best services available.

Each decision maker and each group of stakeholders have a different perspective on the program and tend to interpret results on the basis of personal, professional, and political points of reference. Although stakeholders are important, staff play the primary role in using the evaluation results to enhance the program and to ensure its existence.

No program is safe from the political maneuvering of various stakeholders. However, regularly scheduled program evaluations can help minimize distortions regarding a program's impact and provide hard evidence regarding its effectiveness and viability. Thus, evaluation procedures whose results can be trusted provide hard data and facts to refute negative comments based on political maneuvering. Ongoing program evaluations support a program's creative and innovative activities. Usher (1995) states,

By developing the capacity to monitor and assess their own performance, program managers and staff can risk the mistakes that often
occur with innovation. This is because they can detect problems
and make mid-course corrections before the results of error due to
planning or execution become widely apparent and costly (p. 63).

■ Program and Evaluation Defined

A program and evaluation of a program are not separate
activities. When planned carefully, these two sets of activities can
be integrated into an organized set of ongoing operations that
promote and support each other.

A program is a design of activities that, in theory, produce
some change or outcome in its participants within a given time
frame. How a program works forms its theoretical foundation, and
the practices used to serve the participant represent the application of that theory. In setting goals and objectives, a program specifies standards for success by indicating how much change should
occur in a given time frame. Finally, programs target a given
group of participants in whom desired changes can be noted.

A basic program outcome evaluation measures and describes
outcomes at scheduled points in time. The amount of change in
participants is described in group terms. The success of the program is described in terms of how well the results of an evaluation match the predetermined standards for success. In these
ways, a program defines itself.

The structure of a basic program outcome evaluation is
embedded in the program itself. That is, the program's structure
determines the design and activities of the program's evaluation.
Table 1 outlines the components of program structure and program evaluation.

Table 1. Program Structure and Evaluation Components

Structure	Evaluation
Theory	Design
Practices	Measures and instruments
Goals	Data collection
Objectives	Data analysis
Target population	Results

The evaluation design should be simple and connected directly to the program's objectives. Basic program evaluations consider outcomes as they are measured and provide an overview of the characteristics of the participants included in the evaluation. Because evaluation reports should be considered working documents, recommendations for change, if any are warranted, should be included. Good evaluations do not simply say what happened during the past year; they provide guidance regarding what should happen next year.

■ When to Conduct an Outcome Evaluation

Evaluations should be timed in accordance with two factors: program maturity and time frame for service participants. Outcomes should be measured only after a program has matured to the point at which the first- and second-year "bumps" have been worked out and at the beginning and end of participation by individuals or groups of individuals in the program.

Reporting evaluation results should be timed too. Although information or data collection for an evaluation may be an ongoing process, the actual report, whether an oral presentation or written document, should have a regular "due date." This time frame for reporting results can be quarterly, annually, biannually—whatever time frame seems appropriate for reporting results against the standards of success. In general, the time for participants' completion of the program is a helpful guide for determining how frequently program results should be reported.

■ Outcome Evaluations and Quality Assurance

There are many types of program evaluation: cost effectiveness, process, personnel performance, and others. Each evaluation type focuses on a specific aspect of a program. Quality-assurance evaluations are often confused with program evaluations. Whereas program outcome evaluations look at changes in groups or subgroups of participants, quality-assurance evaluations examine the integrity of a program's procedures, for example, whether participant records are maintained and complete. Agencies often seek licensing and accreditation for their programs and services, which involve quality-assurance evaluations. However, accrediting organizations increasingly require that programs demonstrate effectiveness through program evaluations. Therefore, although quality-assurance and outcome evaluations are somewhat different, the two are often paired. The differences between the two evaluation types are outlined in Table 2.

Table 2. Quality Assurance Evaluation and Program Outcome Evaluation

Evaluation Focus	Quality Assurance Evaluation	Program Outcome Evaluation
Focus	Individual cases	Outcomes
Report	Practices of individual case review	Cases are grouped or aggregated for examination
Basis for Interpretation	Professional judgment and data findings	Data findings

Adapted from Wahl, M., & Maas, F. (1994). *Outcomes for family service agencies.* Paper presented at the 1994 North-Atlantic Conference, Newport, RI.

■ The Evaluator

The evaluator is a person with the skill required to synthesize pieces of information into a larger, more coherent picture; who conducts a follow-up on information; who is able to analyze information by asking good questions in different ways; and who is good with details. The evaluator does not work alone. Staff work with the evaluator to produce a complete and useful evaluation report.

Hiring a professional evaluator should be considered if no staff member has the requisite skills, if program funders require an outside evaluator, and/or if the program evaluation requires sophisticated evaluation tools and methods.

■ Cost of Evaluation

Evaluations cost money and time. Conceptualizing the design and planning the activities constitute the most demanding period of the evaluation. If evaluation activities such as data collection and data analysis are not well planned, they will take more time to implement and complete, and results may be questionable. Thus, it pays to spend sufficient time for the planning stages. Time for basic outcome evaluations can be built into a program's operations. Good evaluations pay for themselves in terms of program growth and development.

Ritual evaluations whose results are ignored are a waste of time and money. Results must be used by staff and administrators. If evaluations are conducted but not used, staff become aggravated, and the program's credibility is put at risk. Evaluations that are performed with integrity and shared with staff as a tool for program improvement and development are cost-effective ways to maintain program viability.

■ Purpose of This Handbook

The purpose of this book is to present an introduction to and overview of basic concepts and methods used in program outcome evaluation. This book is designed for the nonprofessional evaluator who wishes to or has been asked to complete a basic, descriptive outcome evaluation.

To complete such an evaluation on program outcomes, one does not need to be proficient in high-level statistical concepts, although one should have knowledge of the basic descriptive statistics that are presented in this book. The statistics presented in this volume can be performed by hand, although it is assumed that a computer and appropriate software will be available. Calculating statistics by hand provides insight into the meaning of statistical data. The process, however, is cumbersome and can lead to errors. A computer and a statistical software package facilitate accurate results and allow for flexibility in data analysis.

In determining the kind of software package needed, the following may be helpful. For data management, the package should make it easy to enter data, add and delete cases, and add more information to individual cases. For data analysis, the package should include all required analyses for the evaluation, have reader friendly output, and allow the user to select specific subgroups within the data sets for analysis. It is helpful if the package contains some higher level analytic capabilities that look at relationships and differences between groups and variables.

Many of the newer packages offer the point-and-click method for choosing analyses and options. Although entering and analyzing data are work, the point-and-click packages eliminate the frustrations of typos and having to learn rigid rules to complete analyses.

Overview of Concepts

The concepts and procedures presented in this book are necessary components of a basic program outcome evaluation.

Chapter 2 overviews the program components identified in Table 1. Conceptualizing theory and practices and writing goals, objectives, and standards of success help the evaluator identify and define program outcome.

Chapter 3 focuses on the target population, that is, whom the program is designed to serve and who should show change as a result of program participation. The chapter discusses who in the target population should be included in the evaluation study.

Chapters 4 through 7 discuss the activities of the evaluation itself. They present concepts in evaluation design, measurement, data-collection methods, and data analysis.

Chapter 8 focuses on report writing, presenting the basic elements of an evaluation report and executive summary.

Examples

In chapters 2 through 4, four hypothetical programs are used to illustrate concepts. The programs vary according to time required to serve participants, types of target populations, and configuration of program activities. Example 1, Parenting Practices, emphasizes concepts in data collection, analysis, and report writing and is used throughout the book.

> **Example 1:** *Parenting Practices Program.* This is a 10-week program for parents of children who are six years of age or younger. It focuses on discipline and managing behavior and is conducted in a group setting. Parents hear lectures from child experts, are involved in discussions and other interactive activities, and are given practice exercises to try at home with their children.
>
> **Example 2:** *Students at Risk of Dropping Out of School.* This program

is designed for students with a history of truancy and who show signs of dropping out of school. The program is initiated at the beginning of the school year, and students are monitored individually by school counselors according to absenteeism, academic achievement, and self-esteem. Students meet individually with their counselors and in weekly group sessions. Counselors may collaborate with teachers and parents as needed.

Example 3: *Employment Counseling.* This program is designed to counsel participants who have lost their jobs as a result of organization downsizing. Counselors focus on job skills that participants currently possess. The program counsels participants individually, assesses their skills, and keeps them informed on current job listings.

Example 4: *Independent Living for Persons Who Are Mentally Ill.* This program is designed to monitor individuals who have been hospitalized for depression and are currently living alone. A caseworker visits the participant each week, assesses with the participant symptoms of depression, and reviews with colleagues the participant's progress.

"To Do" Lists

Finally, each chapter concludes with a "To Do" list, activities or steps that can be used to complete the design and activities for an evaluation. Here is chapter 1's "To Do" list.

To Do

1. Identify the program to be evaluated.

2. Identify the stakeholder groups that need information about the program's outcomes.

3. Select the evaluator and staff members to work with the evaluator on planning and implementing the evaluation activities.

4. Assess the technical assistance (computer hardware and software) available to complete the evaluation.

References

Joint Commission on Accreditation of Healthcare Organizations. (1992). *1993 accreditation manual for mental health, chemical dependency, and mental retardation/developmental disabilities services* (Vol. 1, standards). Oak Terrace, IL: Author.

Usher, C. L. (1995). Improving evaluability through self-evaluation. *Evaluation Practice, 16*(1), 59–68.

Wahl, M., & Maas, F. (1994). *Outcomes for family service agencies.* Paper presented at the 1994 North-Atlantic Conference, Newport, RI.

2

Defining a Program

Key Terms

Program theory: A framework of assumptions about how a program achieves change in participants.

Program practices: The activities or operations that will produce the expected changes.

Goals: Formal statements, broad in scope, of what a program ideally is intended to achieve.

Outcome: The change observed in a program participant.

Operational definition: Concrete terms or statements used to describe and measure the outcomes.

Objectives: Formal statements of standards of success that indicate how many participants will change, how much change will occur, and the schedule for measuring change.

■ Introduction

When a program is developed, a theoretical foundation for how the program should operate is conceptualized. Goals and objectives are written. Outcomes to be measured are defined. These elements shape the evaluation and outcome-measurement activities. Unfortunately, although many program developers carefully conceptualize a program at the outset, few return to their initially written guidelines when performing an evaluation, relying instead on intuitive knowledge about the program and how it works.

Clearly stated theory, goals, objectives, and operational outcome definitions form the foundation of program evaluation design. In short, success needs to be defined before it can be measured. This means that the program must be described in ways that allow for measurement—describing the program's theory, writing goals and objectives, operationally defining outcomes. The following sections take a step back to review a program's roots and expected achievements.

■ Program Theory

Programs whose objective is to effect change in participants are theory based; that is, the program is based on ideas or assumptions about how the program should change participants. Program theory determines expected outcomes. Bickman (1987) states that program theory "is the construction of a plausible and sensible model of how a program is supposed to work" (p. 5). If the theoretical framework is understood by staff and other stakeholders, the ways in which a program's practices effect change in participants become clear.

How a program works can be captured in a series of "if–then" statements—informal hypothetical statements that link program practices to program effects. These statements of assumptions indicate that *if* something is done to, with, or for program participants for a given period *then* theoretically something will change. If–then statements are, therefore, statements of expectations. The following if–then examples from two of the hypothetical programs described in chapter 1 indicate how these statements might be written.

> **Example 1:** If parents receive training in parenting skills, then parents will learn effective parenting techniques.

> **Example 2:** If students at risk of dropping out of school are counseled and monitored to stay in school and complete their education, then they will not drop out of school.

These examples describe in the *if* statement what will be done to the participants and in the *then* statement how the participants will change.

Although these simple examples describe only one expected change or outcome, many such statements may be devised for any given program. Most programs are multidimensional and complex and have several outcome expectations for participants. For example, the parenting program in example 1 may also expect to increase parents' knowledge in child development and their awareness of child activities in order to enhance the parent–child relationship. The drop-out prevention program may expect to see an increase in academic achievement and self-esteem as well as identification of realistic and positive goals for the at-risk students' future. To get a true picture of a program and its objectives, one should note all expectations using if–then statements. Consequently, it is likely that several such statements will be developed.

Writing such statements requires a careful review to determine whether the *if* statement actually can produce the *then* statement. Sometimes the if–then link is unachievable or sometimes the *if* statement is not adequately related to the *then* statement. This occurs when the program theory or application has been conceptualized poorly, thus creating no change, negative change, or unexpected change among participants. Lipsey and Pollard (1989) state that "a program may be a disappointment because flawed theory was implemented or because a good theory was poorly implemented" (p. 317). Examples 3 and 4 illustrate these mistakes.

> **Example 3 (unachievable):** If job-seeking participants are counseled in the application of their work skills to various careers, then they will be employed.

> **Example 4 (unrelated):** If the mentally ill who are living independently are monitored for depression, then the community will have a greater understanding of depression.

Both of these examples indicate a lack of understanding regarding how the program's activities link with what the program is likely to achieve and suggest poor application of the program's theoretical framework.

In example 3, the program attempts to heighten awareness about job-seeking participants' marketability. Although "being employed" is hoped for, it is not necessarily a direct change or outcome that can be controlled by the program and measured as such. In other words, the expected change is unachievable. In fact, the only change in the participant that one can possibly observe is the participants' increased awareness of employment possibilities, which may be used to find a job. The practices in example 3 are designed to counsel participants in how their work skills may transfer to other careers, not to place the participant into a new job.

To correct this statement, one must determine which side of the statement is true. If the *if* statement is true, then the theoretical framework could be stated as follows: *If* job-seeking participants are counseled in the application of their work skills to various careers, *then* participants will increase their awareness of employment possibilities. If the *then* statement is true, then the theoretical framework can be stated as follows: *if* a job search and interview schedule is implemented for each participation, *then* the participant will be employed.

Example 4 illustrates how if–then statements may not relate to each other. Monitoring depression does not change the community's understanding of the program. If the *if* statement is true the hypothesis might state: *If* the mentally ill who are living independently are monitored for depression, *then* increases in depression levels can be treated more quickly and effectively to allow the participant to continue to live independently. If the *then* side of the statement is true, the statement might read: *If* the program implements an educational campaign on depression and its symptoms, *then* the community will have a greater understanding of depression.

As these examples show, one must look at both sides of theory statements to determine whether program practices and outcomes or expectations match. Examination of *if* statements provides insight into the program practices and answers the question Is this what the program is doing? Examination of *then* statements provides insight into what the program expects to achieve and answers the question Is this what will change in the participant? Finally, examination of the whole statement moves to the heart of the program's theory: Can the program's practices achieve the changes it aims to achieve in participants? The following sections present a more in-depth look at program practices and program goals, providing further insight into defining a program and identifying the theory.

■ Program Practices

Program practices are related to the *if* of the program's theory and answer the question: What does the program do? Practices are program activities designed to achieve a successful outcome. They describe the ways in which staff interact with and monitor participants from program entry to program exit. They are developed to ensure that participants will be positively affected by the program. Practices might include enrollment, assessment, support, counseling, instruction, training, and the like. All staff members follow this map or practice plan with the goal of achieving *program* success—not the success of individual staff members. Generally, these practices, for example, provide instruction, are further defined by the specific activities in which the participant is involved while in the program.

The four program models described below present a basic picture of program practices.

Example 1: If parents receive training in parenting skills, then the parents will learn effective parenting techniques.

Practices: Training in parenting skills.

Practice activities: Lectures, group work and discussion, role play, journal writing, films and videos, parent feedback, etc.

Example 2: If students at risk of dropping out of school are counseled and monitored to stay in school and complete their education, then they will not drop out of school.

Practices: Counsel students to stay in school.

Practice activities: Individual counseling sessions, group sessions, monitoring attendance, goal setting for the future, student feedback, etc.

Example 3: If job-seeking participants are counseled in the application of their work skills to various careers, then participants will recognize the diverse career opportunities open to them.

Practices: Counsel participants about their work skills.

Practice activities: Individual counseling sessions, distribution of job listings, skills assessment, etc.

Example 4: If the mentally ill who are living independently are monitored for depression, then symptoms of depression will be minimized and the participant will continue to live independently.

Practices: Monitor symptoms of depression.

Practice activities: Home visits, observation and recording of behavior, interviews and feedback from participant, weekly reports and recommendations, feedback from supervisor and other professionals, intervention identification and implementation.

The *quality* of these practices should be evaluated separately on a regular basis to examine the consistency and efficiency of a program's practices and operations. Quality-assurance evaluations check the *if* side of the program's theory. Such evaluations, which are beyond the scope of this book, are necessary because inconsistent, inefficient, and low-quality program practices have a direct impact on a program's outcomes. Therefore, program activities must assure quality practices before program outcomes can be measured and described.

Quality-assurance evaluations are usually performed to meet accreditation requirements. Many accrediting organizations now require that an outcome evaluation plan be included in a program's quality-assurance plan.

■ Goals

Goals are direct statements of the *then* focus of a program's theory. Goals answer the question: What does the program hope to achieve? Goals are broad statements of outcomes and provide direction for outcomes. In most programs, goals are probably the most readily available aspect of the program. They are frequently written in grants, program literature, five-year plans, and so forth. But many evaluations begin and stop with the stated goals because people often view goals as defined outcomes. In most programs, however, this is not the case. Goals sometimes use all-encompassing language that captures many outcomes. Some goals are considered an ideal program achievement rather than a realistic statement of what can actually be achieved. Thus, goals generally do not precisely identify or define a measurable outcome.

Using the four examples, program goals are stated and outcomes noted. As can be seen, goal statements capture the heart of the program, but are necessarily broad. Goals are often used to market a program and can sometimes have as many interpretations as there are readers.

> **Example 1:** If parents receive training in parenting skills, then the parents will learn effective parenting techniques.
>
> *Goal: Parents will understand effective parenting practices.*
>
> *Outcome: Increased knowledge of successful parenting techniques.*
>
> **Example 2:** If students at risk of dropping out of school are counseled and monitored to stay in school and complete their education, then they will not drop out of school.
>
> *Goal: At-risk students will complete school successfully.*
>
> *Outcome: Absenteeism will be decreased, student status continued, grades improved.*

Example 3: If job-seeking participants are counseled in the application of their work skills to various careers, then participants will recognize the diverse career opportunities open to them.

Goal: Job seekers will recognize career opportunities.

Outcomes: Increased awareness of employment opportunities, identification of transferable job skills.

Example 4: If the mentally ill who are living independently are monitored for depression, then symptoms of depression will be minimized and the participant will continue to live independently.

Goal: The mentally ill will continue to live independently.

Outcome: Depression symptoms will be minimized and independent living status maintained.

Examples 1, 2, and 3 have straightforward goals and identified outcomes. Example 4 is more complex in that a change in depression level, in this program, actually activates another type of program practice—intervention to treat the depression. This program's purpose is to monitor for depression until intervention is necessary. Its success is determined by what *does not* happen to the participant—increase in depression and the need to place the participant in a care facility.

In each of these four examples, only one goal was noted. However, these programs may be expected to achieve several changes in participants and thus are likely to have more than one goal. Goals are broad statements and can include more than one outcome, as examples 2 and 4 illustrate.

■ Outcomes

Although goals offer the first glimpse of outcomes, they do not indicate precisely what will be measured. The next step in describing a program is to define what is meant by each outcome or what will be measured and what the program must do to achieve success or how the outcome will be measured. These definitions of outcomes, to be measurable, must be observed in some way. This means that the participant must undergo change that can be observed and measured. For example, the parenting program's outcome is *an increase in effective parenting techniques*. In this outcome, effective parenting techniques need to be operationally defined. It is known that increased knowledge will be the measure of success in this program, because program practices include instruction or training in effective parenting techniques.

Operational Definitions

Operational definitions are concrete statements that describe outcomes in a way that can be observed and measured. The operational definition is the context in which the terms used to identify the outcomes are understood by staff and all other stakeholders (Creswell, 1994). "An operational definition specifies the activities . . . that will serve as indicators" of the outcome being measured (Anastas & MacDonald, 1994, p. 54).

Operational definitions can be developed by staff to fit the unique aspects of the program. However, these definitions must also be credible in relation to other existing definitions that have been developed (e.g., in the literature) and practiced in the program's activities. For example, an observed behavior of absenteeism would not be credible if it were defined as the ability to play basketball. This, of course, is an extreme example of a definition that does not fit; the point is that the definition must have some basis of credibility.

The definition, however, does not have to be absolute. Few operational definitions are absolute. Operational definitions may be narrowed or constricted by program practices. They may not be "ultimate representations of a concept" (Babbie, 1973, p. 134) but rather representations of part of a concept that creates the program's focus. Programs, by design, narrow or constrict their focus to that which is achievable among participants.

Operational definitions are necessary because "words of everyday language are rich in meaning" (Creswell, 1994, p. 106) and outcomes without an operational definition may be understood in different ways by different staff members and groups of stakeholders. Further, outcomes can be understood in different ways by the same people or groups at different times in the program's cycle of activities. In short, if staff and other stakeholders do not have an operational definition to which they may return from time to time, they are likely to disagree about what the outcome is, about what should be measured, and, worse, about what is measured and presented in the final report. If this happens, the program's credibility can be jeopardized.

Sometimes an outcome cannot be defined in operational or behavioral terms. Babbie (1973) states that an operational definition "specifies . . . observations that may be taken as indicators" of the outcome (p. 134). This means that with some outcomes, behaviors that are observable and measurable may only *indicate* the outcome. This is especially true of elusive outcomes such as self-esteem, identity, and depression.

In these instances, a list of observable behaviors is used as the operational definition to provide direction in measuring outcome.

Examine the operational definitions in the following four examples:

> **Example 1:** Parenting techniques are defined as identified effective methods of discipline, such as time outs, setting rules, identifying consequences, etc.

> **Example 2:** Absenteeism is defined as not present in school two or more hours during a regularly scheduled school day. Student status is defined as active enrollment with a schedule of classes.

> **Example 3:** Employment opportunities are defined as jobs that are applicable to an identified job skill.

> **Example 4:** Depression symptoms are defined as behaviors that indicate lack of self-care such as hygiene, keeping appointments, taking medication, etc. Independent living is defined as living without continuous medical or mental health care such as hospitalization, adult foster care, etc.

Each of these definitions limits the scope of the outcome. Further, each of these definitions is measurable in some way because it can be directly observed.

Objectives

Objectives are formal statements of a program's expected and measured achievements. Objectives state the standards for success to which the evaluation results will be compared.

Two types of standards are written into objectives. According to Rossi and Freeman (1993), objectives may have either absolute or relative standards for success. An absolute standard for success requires that an "undesirable condition be totally eliminated or that a desired one may be attained for everyone. Relative [standards], in contrast, establish standards of achievement in terms of some proportionate improvement in existing conditions" (p. 113).

Absolute objective standards can be unrealistic and un-achievable, particularly for programs directed toward high-risk populations and/or that have high drop-out rates. Relative objective standards are more reasonable and usually more realistic. However, determining a relative standard for success can be tricky because it requires knowledge of program participants' behavior. Such factors as drop-out rate, length of program, and so forth, need to be considered before setting the standard in a program. Standards that are set too high can set the stage for failure; standards set too low lack significance.

The objectives for the four examples used throughout this chapter are presented in relative terms. In each instance, only a proportion of the participants are expected to succeed on the measure of change within the program's time frame.

> **Example 1:** When given a list of parenting practices, at least 70% of the parents will show an increase of 20 or more points between their pretest and posttest scores.

> **Example 2:** Compared with the absentee rate of the same month of the previous school year, at least 40% of the students will show a decrease of three or more days of absenteeism each month.

> **Example 3:** When given a list of job descriptions, at least 80% of the participants will select a minimum of three employment opportunities in which they possess job skills that qualify them for a job that is described.

> **Example 4:** Using a depression-behavior checklist, the home outreach worker will observe that 50% or more of the participants are maintaining or decreasing their level of depression as specified in the participant's treatment plan over each six-week monitoring period.

All these objectives include three important standards or expected results: (1) the minimum percent of participants who will show the change in the expected outcome, (2) the minimum amount of change expected, and (3) the time frame in which change will be measured. Table 3 shows how the objectives fit into each of the standards.

Percent of Participants Who Will Change

The percent of participants who complete the program and will show change is based on the number of persons who enroll in the program and participate in the program activities. This percent represents the minimum number of participants who will show expected change. Of course, a greater percentage of participants may succeed.

Change Expected

Expected change indicates the direction of the change—increase, decrease, maintain—and the minimum amount of change that should be observed. Participants, of course, may show that they have exceeded the amount of change expected.

Measuring Points

For change to be observed, a condition or behavior must be different in some way from a previous condition or behavior. This means that before a participant became active in the program and was exposed to the program's effects, the participant did not possess the desired outcome. Therefore, a premeasure or pretest is given to determine where the participant is when he or she begins the program. The results of this measure are compared with the results of the posttest administered upon completion of the program (or some other designated point) to determine the amount of change that has occurred.

Table 3. Common Standards of Success for the Example Objectives

	Percent of participants to change	Least amount of change expected	Measuring points
Objective 1	70%	20-point or more increase in score	Pretest/posttest
Objective 2	40%	3 days' decrease in absenteeism per month	Previous year (pretest); current year (posttest)
Objective 3	80%	3 jobs identified	Pretest/posttest
Objective 4	50% with no change	Maintain or decrease level of depression	Repeated measure every six weeks beginning with first visit and ending at termination

■ Summary

This chapter presents a brief overview of the various conceptual components of program outcome evaluation. Defining outcomes, operations, and standards of success are key to developing good programs that can be measured. Program evaluation is rooted in these elements. Program theory, program practices, and goals provide direction for the evaluation, and operationally defined outcomes that are observable and measurable focus the evaluation activities.

To Do

1. Write *if–then* statements to show how the program works. Use the *if* side to describe program practices. Use the *then* side to describe the change or outcome that participants will show. Examine the statements to determine whether the practices match the changes or outcomes.

2. Using the *if* statements, separately list the program activities.

3. Use the *then* statements to develop goals or broad statements of the program's purpose.

4. Identify all outcomes that might be included under the goal.

5. For each outcome, write in concrete terms an operational definition that can be measured.

6. For each outcome, write an objective that identifies the program's standards for success. Include the percent of participants who will show change, the minimum amount of change to be observed, and the points of measurement used to note change.

References

Anastas, J., & MacDonald, M. (1994). *Research design for social work and the human services.* New York: Lexington Books.

Babbie, E. (1973). *Survey research methods.* Belmont, CA: Wadsworth.

Bickman, L. (Ed.). (1987). Using program theory in evaluation. *New Directions for Program Evaluation, 33*(1), 5–18.

Creswell, J. (1994). *Research design.* Thousand Oaks, CA: Sage Publications.

Lipsey, M. W., & Pollard, J. A. (1989). Driving toward theory in program evaluation: More models to choose from. *Evaluation and Program Planning, 12,* 317–328.

Rossi, P. H., & Freeman, H. E. (1993). *Evaluation: A systematic approach.* Newbury Park, CA: Sage Publications.

3
Target Population

Key Terms

Target population: The group or groups of participants for which the program has been designed. All members of the target population share one or more characteristics such as gender, marital status, educational background, etc.

Program participants: Members of the target population who have enrolled and taken part in program activities.

Program completers: Participants who have met all the program requirements.

■ Introduction

Programs often serve various groups with the goal of initiating multiple changes. However, most programs target according to specific characteristics the groups they intend to serve. These characteristics—gender, marital status, educational background, and so forth—describe the target population.

These group characteristics must be kept in mind while developing a program and its operations and activities. With regard to program evaluation, these characteristics are considered to determine who among the participants will be included in the evaluation study. This chapter discusses defining the target population and determining what participants among the target population should be included in the evaluation study.

■ Defining the Target Population

A target population is the group for which the program has been designed. Potential participants are identified by common characteristics that fit the program's structure and activities and that are shared by all potential participants. According to Scriven (1991), the "intended consumer" is the target population.

It is important to define the target population's characteristics clearly so that program theory, practice, and outcomes can be developed accordingly. For example, it doesn't make sense to plan a parenting program dealing with issues of parenting children of all ages if the target population is parents of young children. The focus of the program can determine the characteristics of the population, or, conversely, the program may be developed to respond to the needs of a particular group of potential participants.

The target population, then, is the group of potential participants who are most likely to show expected outcome gains. Good program theory identifies the target population by taking its characteristics into account. Rossi and Freeman (1993) include basic characteristics such as social and demographic criteria, geographic location, life difficulties, and life conditions. Other kinds of characteristics include the following:

- *Gender*
- *Age:* Specific age group, age range, developmental stage of life, for example, preschoolers, early adolescents, elderly senior citizens, etc. If such terms are to identify program participants, they should specify the actual age range. Preschoolers may or may not include toddlers. If mental age is used, intelligence is generally assessed.
- *Race:* A program may be developed around the cultural issues of a particular racial or ethnic group.
- *Marital status:* For example, single parents, widowed within the past five years, twice divorced, and the like.
- *Education level:* For example, fewer than nine years of formal schooling, without a high school diploma, high school diploma, two years or less of post–high school education, and so forth.
- *Intelligence:* A program may be designed for gifted students or for individuals who are educable but mentally handicapped. Generally, IQ tests or other intelligence-assessment tests are used to identify these groups.
- *Achievement:* Programs may focus on groups of individuals who have achieved a level of knowledge in a particular area, such as math, life skills, etc.
- *Drinking behavior:* A program may be designed for participants who consume a certain number of ounces of alcohol a day. In this program the actual amount of alcohol consumed per day may be specified.

These are only a few of the kinds of characteristics that may be considered in a target population. Programs may focus on a combination of characteristics as well. For example, a pregnancy-prevention program may be designed for adolescent boys, wherein age (adolescent) and gender (male) are participant characteristics. The program might require other eligibility characteristics by designating whether the adolescent boy is already a father. Depending on the operational definition of prevention, the program may be designed to prevent additional pregnancies rather than first pregnancies.

Target populations are generally mentioned, sometimes vaguely and sometimes specifically, in theory statements, goals, and objectives. Regardless how they are mentioned, they need to be defined separately as well. Target population definitions are similar in structure to operational definitions of outcomes in that they define the eligibility of a potential participant in a given program. In the four example programs, identification of the target population is obtained from the goal statement, then defined.

Example 1

Goal: Parents will understand effective parenting practices.

Definition: The target population is parents of children six years of age or younger.

Example 2

Goal: At-risk students will complete school successfully.

Definition: The target population is students at risk of dropping out of school and defined further as students enrolled in grades six through eight between the ages of 11 and 14 years. At-risk students should have a three-year or longer history of absenteeism of 40 or more days per year prior to entering the program.

Example 3

Goal: Job seekers will recognize career opportunities.

Definition: The target population participants have lost their job as a result of organizational restructuring in the past six months.

Example 4

Goal: The mentally ill will continue to live independently.

Definition: The target population is mentally ill persons 65 years of age and older who live independently and have been hospitalized for depression within the past year. These individuals are taking medication to control depression symptoms and receive government assistance.

These examples show a wide range of target population criteria or eligibility characteristics. One should be clear about the characteristics of the population served by the program. The structure and the activities of the program are influenced by the way in which the target population is defined.

Some programs, however, may define the target population in general terms. For example, a tutoring center at a community college may be open to all students who request a tutor, even if the request is one time only and for 10 minutes. Thus, this target population would have only one characteristic criterion—an active student at the college. The program includes all types of students with any need. Rossi and Freeman (1993) state that it is risky to be too inclusive in defining a population because doing so might result in poor program-planning decisions. Evaluations from such programs may need to define groups within the target population further and look at the results of these groups separately. In the community-college tutoring program, a breakdown of results might consider frequency of use among the students, specifying frequent users, occasional users, one-time users, and so forth. How a student uses the service is defined as specifically as possible.

By specifying subgroups of the target population, staff are able to gain a better understanding about how the program affects specific groups within the target population. How various target population groups perform helps point out where and when changes in program activities are needed. Evaluations often break out the various target populations to provide insight into the program's performance.

Example 1: The target population is parents of young children. However, the program may also wish to examine the program's effects on households with a single parent, with two parents, and with other parenting structures.

Example 2: The target population is students at risk of dropping out of school. This program may want to look at the program's impact on male participants and female participants or it may want to look at students in sixth grade and students in eighth grade.

Example 3: The target population is job seekers. This program may want to look at different age ranges within its target populations, such as job seekers younger than 30 years of age; job seekers between 30 and 45 years old; and job seekers older than 45.

Example 4: The target population is mentally ill persons who are living independently. This program may also wish to analyze groups on the basis of their hospital discharge date and the number of months since leaving the hospital or perhaps the types of medication the participant is taking to control depression.

The groups within the target population should be clearly defined and considered to be significant for evaluation and study. These subgroups are considered significant if their results are likely to vary and be a cause for consideration when the program results are interpreted. Therefore, it is important to identify these groups before the data are collected for the evaluation.

■ Defining the Program Participant

In addition to defining the target population, one must also define program participants. Each participant, before being included in an evaluation study, should be reviewed on two levels: his or her membership in the target population and his or her program-activity status.

Target-Population Membership

Not all program participants should be considered eligible for an evaluation study. Every program has a few participants who do not meet eligibility requirements. Realistically, programs often enroll or include some nontarget population participants because of special needs and considerations and a belief that the program may benefit these individuals in some way. It is not wrong to include them. However, these exceptions to the target population can distort evaluation results. Participants who are not members of the target population may be affected by the program's structure and activities differently from other participants. The program utilizes the characteristics of the target population to structure program operations and activities. Nontarget population participants might show outcomes that are not typical of the target population. If the nontarget population results are mixed with the target population results, the program's impact on participants may not be accurately reflected. In such cases, decisions regarding program changes might be made unnecessarily and inappropriately.

In an evaluation study, nontarget population participants should be considered in one of two ways: They should be eliminated from the evaluation study if they are few or if reporting their results might breach confidentiality, or their results should be reported separately from those of the target population. Their status as nontarget population participants should be noted in the final report.

Program-Activity Status

Program-activity status is based on the amount of time the participant has invested in a program. Programs are structured according to how much time it takes to initiate change among participants. Consequently, a program should report results on participants who have completed all or most of the activities of the program because these participants (program completers) are the "true consumers of the program" (Scriven, 1991, p. 190).

Program completers are identified through attendance records maintained in billing statements, sign-ins, and so forth. These records also indicate other types of participants:

- *Continuing participant:* This participant has not been in the program long enough to be considered a completer and is likely to be included in the next round of evaluation activities. Continuing participants are found in programs that are run in multiple, overlapping series. To determine whether a continuing participant is eligible for evaluation, his or her attendance record should be reviewed for completion of the program.

- *Occasional attender:* An occasional attender is a participant whose attendance and participation are erratic. His or her absence may be caused by various circumstances, from lack of transportation to lack of commitment. Before the evaluation is initiated, one should determine the number of activities required to categorize a participant as a program completer or as an occasional attender. In some programs, one missed activity might identify a participant as an occasional attender. The program's theory, goals, and objectives guide this decision.

- *Dropouts:* A participant is considered a dropout if he or she leaves the program before meeting its time-in-program requirement. In some programs, particularly long-term programs, the participant needs to be officially declared a dropout so that he or she is not categorized as an occasional attender and a dropout at the same time.

- *Suspension:* In rare instances, a participant may be asked to leave the program before completing the required time-in-program requirement.
- *No show:* A participant is a no show if he or she has enrolled in a program but has not attended any scheduled activity. Follow-up calls may need to be made. Other categories unique to a given program may need to be devised, and the categories listed above do not apply to all programs. For example, in a drop-in tutoring program, the no-show category does not apply, and a drug-rehabilitation program may not allow occasional attendance and consider all participants who miss a scheduled activity as suspended from the program.

In addition to looking at the attendance records of participants who complete the program, it is advantageous to compare the patterns of attendance of the other participant categories—continuing, occasional, dropouts, etc.—against the program's scheduled activities. When do participants begin to miss activities or drop out? Are some activities skipped more often than others? Evaluating these results will allow staff to determine the following:

- Where attendance drops among continuing participants
- What activities attract occasional participants
- At what point dropouts are likely to stop attending the program
- What activities appear to be least attractive to participants

Attendance patterns should be evaluated over time. A particular group's patterns do not necessarily reflect patterns among other groups at other times.

Trends emerge after the program has been implemented several times. In evaluating trends, staff have the opportunity to adjust the program's practices and schedule of activities to encourage attendance and participation.

■ Summary

Determining the eligibility of program participants in an evaluation study is a twofold task. First, participants should be reviewed on the basis of all target population characteristics. A program's structure and activities are guided by these characteristics. Second, participant attendance is important in determining whether an individual is a consumer of the program's services.

To Do

1. Define the target population.
2. Identify subgroups within the target populations that should be considered during analysis.
3. Establish participant categories based on program attendance requirements.

References

Rossi, P. H., & Freeman, H. E. (1993). *Evaluation: A systematic approach.* Newbury Park, CA: Sage Publications.
Scriven, M. (1991). *Evaluation thesaurus* (4th ed.) Newbury Park, CA: Sage Publications.

4

Evaluation Design

Key Terms

Evaluation design: The plan of activities or methods that guide the evaluation process.

Data collection: The process and time line through which information is gathered.

Instrument: The tool used to measure the outcomes.

Data analysis: The way information is evaluated to obtain the results.

Data point: Designated time(s) during the course of the program when data are collected.

Sustained effects: Measured outcomes after participants exit the program.

■ Introduction

The design of a program outcome evaluation study is driven by a simple question: Did the program meet its expected standards of success? In designing a program evaluation, one identifies the most efficient methods and procedures to be followed while performing an evaluation (Scriven, 1991). Elements of the design are already reflected in the program theory and practices. Operational definitions specify what will be measured, and the description of the target population indicates who will be measured. Some elements of the design are described in the program objectives, which specify when a measure or measures will be performed on the target population.

Stating the design is a way to formalize the evaluation. In general, the design may be considered an action plan; most programs include a description of the design in their quality-assurance plans. This formal statement includes various procedural statements to guide the evaluation activities:

- What outcomes will be measured.
- Who will be measured.
- When the outcomes will be measured.
- How the outcomes will be measured.
- How the outcomes will be analyzed and reported.

Chapters two and three presented information on what outcomes will be measured and who will be measured, respectively. This chapter looks at how the evaluation design is used to specify times when the outcomes will be measured. Subsequent chapters will look at how the outcomes will be measured, analyzed, and reported.

■ Describing the Design

Designs should be presented in a written format outlining the appropriate times when outcomes should be measured. It is also helpful to illustrate the time line, particularly if data collection is complex or if various outcomes will be measured. A description of the evaluation design is often required in quality-assurance plans and is a useful document for program staff who are responsible for measuring outcomes.

The data-collection schedule arises out of the program's theory and practices. The evaluation design designates times when information on outcomes is gathered from participants. These times are called data points. The number of data points in a design is indicated by the number of times an outcome is measured.

Program theory, practices, and objectives are used to determine when change in participants is likely to occur. The evaluation design indicates the points in the program's time line when measures on the outcomes will be taken. Program objectives generally state how participants will change. How this change will be measured is planned for in advance of the actual task of data collection. Therefore, scheduling of data collection is defined, in part, by the staff's understanding where participants are when they begin the program and where participants are at various points in the program or when they complete the program.

To note change, a design must take at least two measures on outcomes. Thus a design will have a minimum of two data points—the classic pretest/posttest design. In this design the first data point is scheduled before the participant participates in the program's activities (pretest). Most programs use assessment, screening, or diagnostic tools to establish a baseline measurement of participants before they enter the program.

The second data point in the pretest/posttest design is usually scheduled immediately after the participant has completed the program. The posttest is measured the same way as the pretest is measured.

Because the posttest repeats the pretest, this design is sometimes referred to as a *repeated-measure design*. It is important to use the same measure (or an allowable alternative) at both the pretest and posttest data points (see chapter 5).

The posttest measure is relatively easy to schedule: Generally it is taken during the last session or time in which the participant is actively involved in the program. The difference in scores can be calculated from the pretest and posttest data. (The calculation of the change will be discussed in chapter 7.)

This schedule of data collection can be illustrated as follows:

$$X1 \text{————————————————————} X2$$

Pretest	Posttest
(Entry into program)	(Exit from program)

$X1$ = The first data point or the pretest
—— = The time in the program after which
a participant is expected to show change
$X2$ = The second data point or the posttest

Some programs, however, may wish to evaluate participants' progress at various points throughout the program. In examples 2 and 4—the students at risk and the independent living programs—the program objectives indicate that more than two data points will be scheduled. These programs need to measure the progress of participants at various points in the program in order to monitor participants and track outcomes. Some conditions whereby program designers may wish to establish more than two data points in a repeated-measures design include:

- A need to monitor participants closely.
- Program requires an interim report.
- Program requires a long-term commitment from participants and tracking of outcomes over time.

- Program attempts to achieve extensive change in a short period.
- Program is in a state of development, and the amount of time in which to expect change is unknown. A design with three repeated measures would look like the following:

Repeated-Measures Design

X1 ———————————— X2 ———————————— X3

Entry into program   Exit from the program

  X1 = The first data point or the pretest
  X2 = The second data point or the interim measure
  X3 = The third data point or the posttest change

When interim data points are scheduled, corresponding objectives and standards of success should be stated for these points.

The four example programs are described and illustrated with the program's outcome objective used as a guide to identify times for measuring change.

Example 1
 Objective: When given a list of parenting practices, 70% or more parents will increase their pretest score by 20 or more points on the posttest.

 Evaluation design: This program uses a pretest/posttest design. The outcome will be measured before the participant takes part in any program activities (pretest) and again after the activities of the last scheduled program session (posttest). Differences in scores between pretest and posttest will be obtained.

Pretest/Posttest Design of Parenting Program

X1 ——————————————————————————— X2

  X1 = Pretest before parenting program activities begin
  X2 = Posttest after last scheduled activity is completed

Example 2
 Objective: When compared with the absentee rate in the same month of the previous year, 40% or more of the students will show a decrease in absenteeism by three days each month.

Evaluation design: This design requires a repeated measure. The outcome of absenteeism of each student in the program is measured on the last school day of each month from September through June. Differences between the current month's absentee rate and the absentee rate of the same month of the prior year will be examined.

Repeated-Measures Design of Student-at-Risk Program
X1—X2—X3—X4—X5—X6—X7—X8—X9—X10
X1 = September
X2 = October
X3 = November
X4 = December
X5 = January
X6 = February
X7 = March
X8 = April
X9 = May
X10 = June

Example 3

Objective: When given a list of job descriptions, 80% of the participants will select at least three employment opportunities in which they possess job skills that qualify them for a position.

Evaluation design: This a pretest/posttest design. The outcome will be measured on each participant prior to any career counseling and again after the last counseling session. Differences in the scores between the pretest and posttest will be examined.

Pretest/Posttest Design of Employment Program
X1 ——————————————— X2
X1 = Pretest before program counseling activities
X2 = Posttest after last counseling activity

Example 4

Objective: Using a depression behavior checklist, the home outreach worker will observe that 50% or more of the participants will maintain or decrease their level of depression as specified in their treatment plan over each six-week monitoring period.

Evaluation design: Over the period the participant is being monitored by the program, depression symptoms will be observed every six weeks and compared with the most recent observations for changes.

Repeated-Measures Design of Independent Living Program
$X1$—$X2$—$X3$—$X4$—Xn
$X1$ = First 6 weeks
$X2$ = Second 6 weeks
$X3$ = Third 6 weeks
$X4$ = Fourth 6 weeks
Xn = Continue until participant exits program

■ Sustained Effects

Evaluators may be asked to report the *sustained effects* of the program. Sustained effect is the measurement result of the outcome after some designated period after exiting the program. Sustained effects indicate whether program participants sustain change after leaving the program and are not exposed to program activities. Essentially, evaluation of sustained effects asks whether the participant lost, gained, or stayed the same since the last outcome measure. Such follow-ups provide relevant information regarding the strengths and weaknesses in the program's theory, practices, and impact on the participant. How much time should pass before a sustained effects measure is taken?

Example 1

Follow-up: Six weeks after the program ends, parents will be asked to complete the posttest to determine whether their score on parenting skills has remained the same, increased, or decreased.

Example 2

Follow-up: Throughout the year after participants exit the program their absenteeism will be monitored monthly to determine if their absentee rates have changed in any way.

Example 3

Follow-up: Six months after exiting the program, participants will be contacted to determine if they are working and/or applying for work in a profession different from their original career choice.

Example 4

Follow-up: Twelve weeks after termination from the program, participants will be contacted to determine whether their living status and level of depression have changed.

Follow-up measures can help validate the effectiveness of a program. However, problems occur in undertaking a sustained-effects evaluation study. Evaluators have little control over what has happened to the participant between exiting the program and the follow-up study. Various events in the lives of participants during this time frame can have a significant impact on the sustained effect of the program, and evaluators may lack sufficient information about these events and how they might influence the sustained effect. Such events for the four examples might be:

> **Example 1:** Enrollment in additional parenting courses, reading parenting books, joining parenting support groups
>
> **Example 2:** Illness, suspension, transfer out of and back into the school
>
> **Example 3:** Family responsibilities, economic climate, additional courses
>
> **Example 4:** Physical illness, eviction from home, change in income

Evaluators may also experience difficulties finding participants after they have left the program. Although loss of a few participants may not present problems, in many social and educational programs, the target population may be highly transient. Participants may move or refuse to participate, thereby weakening the results of a follow-up study. Consequently, such studies are difficult to undertake, and the consultation of a professional evaluator may be necessary.

■ Information to Collect

After determining *when* data will be collected, evaluators must determine *what* data will be collected. Collecting data for evaluation studies does not necessarily have to be extra work, because in most programs, data on individual participants are collected on an ongoing basis. Such records include enrollment or intake forms, tests, payment records, sign-in records, and the like. Although such information may be collected for other purposes, it can also serve as sources of data for the evaluation. Three types of quantitative data commonly collected in outcome evaluations are often available in individual participant records: outcomes, demographic information, and attendance.

Outcome Data

As discussed in chapter 2, outcomes are the result of measuring the program's objectives as determined by the operational definition of the program. An outcome is observed or measured change in a program participant.

Demographic Data

Background information or demographic data can be very helpful in evaluating outcomes. In chapter 3 common characteristics for the target population were listed and defined. Breaking down these characteristics into subgroups can provide information on the make-up of the program's participants. By breaking out subgroups, evaluators obtain important information about the program's performance that can be used to make adjustments in the program. From these subgroups, specific questions may be identified. Answers to these questions may yield additional demographic data for the evaluation study. In the example programs, the following "subquestions" might be identified.

Example 1
- Do single parents score 20 points or more on the posttest?
- Do partnered parents score 20 points or more on the posttest?

For this program, household-parenting status provides additional information for the evaluation study.

Example 2
- What are the monthly attendance outcomes for females?
- What are the monthly attendance outcomes for males?

For this program, gender provides additional information for the evaluation study.

Example 3
- How do the job seekers younger than 30 years of age score?
- How do job seekers between 30 and 45 years old score?
- How do job seekers older than 45 score?

For this program, participant age provides additional demographic information useful to the evaluation study.

Example 4
- What is the level of depression for participants who are living independently for the first time after six weeks?
- What is the level of depression for participants who are living independently for the first time after 12 weeks?

For this program, date of release from the hospital is relevant information for the evaluation study.

A program evaluation design may include subgroups that are not considered critical to the program's target population. However, these subgroups may be relevant to the program's success. For example, a program may not be gender specific, but staff may nevertheless want to determine whether males are doing as well as females are.

Attendance

For billing purposes, proof of participation, utilization review, and so forth, most programs keep attendance records on individual participants. The attendance record of a participant is also used to determine eligibility in the evaluation study. In chapter 3, five types of participants were described: program completer, continuing participant, occasional attender, dropout, and no show. These types are defined by their attendance records.

Another way to look at outcomes is by attendance group. For example, evaluators may want to compare the outcomes of program completers with those of occasional attenders.

■ Program Maturity

Programs go through developmental stages. Newly implemented programs must work out glitches and kinks. Older, more established programs must refine and monitor their population in order to make necessary adjustments. Therefore, before initiating any evaluation activity, the maturity of a program should be considered to determine the kind of evaluation activities that can be performed—formative or summative.

Formative Evaluation

Newly implemented programs are likely to have some bumps to smooth out. One should not attempt to measure outcomes or program effects while in the midst of working out a program's kinks. In the very early stages of program implementation, program evaluation looks at how a program is forming.

Results from a formative evaluation are used primarily by program developers, administration, and staff to guide decisions intended to improve program performance (Scriven, 1991). Formative evaluation provides program personnel with feedback on program practices to help them work out rough spots and to determine whether that which was conceptualized on paper is consistent with expected outcomes. Therefore, at this point data collection is performed on a trial basis, and information derived from it cannot be used if the program will subsequently change or its practices are modified. Results from a formative evaluation provide initial evidence of the program's ability to achieve success by identifying the strength of relationship between practices and outcomes. Shadis, Cook, and Leviton (1991) note that results from "formative evaluations improve program performance" because results influence "immediate decisions about the program, especially about how its component parts and processes could be improved" (p. 59).

A formative evaluation should answer several questions about the program:

- Is the program serving the target population adequately and appropriately?
- Are the measures appropriate?
- Is the program working toward the desired outcomes?

After a program has been determined to be running smoothly and ready for an outcome evaluation, then the designs as described earlier in this chapter would be implemented.

Summative Evaluation

After a program has matured and its bumps have been smoothed out, a summative evaluation is conducted. Shadish and colleagues (1991) note that "summative evaluations judge program worth by assessing program effects" (p. 59). Summative evaluations examine program outcomes and determine how well objective criteria have been met. These evaluations assume that practices have been examined for appropriateness and that the program is established and working at its full potential. Any evaluation of program practices at this time is a quality-assurance evaluation.

Mature programs measure outcomes. Regularly scheduled outcome evaluations provide information about the program's performance over time. Yearly results can be used to identify cyclical patterns to judge whether the program is meeting its objectives, to monitor changes in its population and participants' needs, and to formalize any shift from the program's intended direction.

A summative evaluation should answer several questions about the program.

- Is the program successful at meeting its objectives?
- Is the program doing as well as it has done in past years?
- Are shifts in the target population evident?

Although summative evaluation results should be used by all stakeholder groups, the results are particularly relevant to program staff because results provide insight into the effectiveness of their work.

■ Summary

This chapter described the evaluation design—when to collect data and what data to collect. It is critically important to schedule data collection for times when participants are active in the program. Data collection schedules are linked directly to the duration of the program. Most programs require a repeated-measure design to determine the amount of change in participants. Length of program, intensity of the program, and the need to monitor participants closely make it necessary to take interim measures on outcomes.

Some subgroups in the target population may be of such importance to a program that they may need to be evaluated. The desired data related to these subgroups should be identified in the design of a program so they can be included in the data-collection process.

Finally, the level of program maturity is an important consideration in program evaluation. New programs look at practices and pilot test the evaluation methods; mature programs undergo quality-assurance evaluations as well as measure and describe outcomes as determined by the design.

To Do

1. Using program objectives, identify data points.

2. Write a description of the evaluation design. Illustate the design by noting measures of the outcomes and the points in time when the measure will be taken.

3. Determine the maturity of the program and either pilot the design or implement it.

References

Scriven, M. (1991). *Evaluation thesaurus* (4th ed.) Newbury Park, CA: Sage Publications.

Shadish, Jr., W. R., Cook, T. D., & Leviton, L. C. (1991). *Foundations of program evaluation.* Newbury park, CA: Sage Publications.

5

Tools to Measure Outcomes

Key Terms

Quantitative tools: Instruments that use numerical values as a measure of outcome.

Qualitative tools: Instruments that use descriptions and detailed perceptions as a measure of outcome. Qualitative measures often enhance and add to an operational definition.

Standardized instrument: A tool that uses the same procedures for administering, scoring, and interpreting results of that which is being observed.

■ Introduction

Outcomes must be measured with an instrument or tool designed to capture change in program participants. Such tools come in many forms but they must always measure the outcome as defined by the operational definition. Various measurement tools include short-answer response categories, surveys, observations, interviews, and so forth. Some of these tools are used to capture specific information, whereas others may be used to capture a rich overview of information.

This chapter examines quantitative measuring tools, that is, short responses that measure specific or fixed information that relates directly to the operational definition. In previous chapters, discussion of the operational definition stated that it must be observed or measurable. Quantitative measures use numerical values to quantify the outcomes and later to calculate the amount of change observed in program participants. The chapter concludes with a discussion of the use of qualitative measures, that is, open-ended measures that elaborate on and interpret quantitative results.

■ Quantitative Measures

Quantitative measures present results as numerical values. Scriven (1991) defines such measures as the "determination of the magnitude of the quantity" (p. 226). Response-category measures that require paper and pencil to complete—either by the program participant or by the staff worker who is observing the participant—are most familiar. Results from these measures can be collected from many program participants, analyzed, and reported in a relatively short period. Results allow for simple tracking of information over time.

Quantitative measures require little time and are cost effective. They can be easily integrated into program operations and generally can be administered by any staff member. Most stakeholders require results from quantitative measures because they perceive such data to be the most credible measure of change.

Quantitative measures have disadvantages, however. Such measures are limited by the numerical values they provide. Anastas and MacDonald (1994) state that the "phenomenon of interest [the outcome] will be defined or delimited by what they can capture" (p. 115). In other words, other than numbers showing that change has occurred, quantitative measures provide no information to enhance or explain the change. They cannot provide information on how the participant perceives the change or explain to what the participant attributes the change. Quantitative measurement is sometimes referred to as the "black box" method of evaluation because it measures what the participant looked like before the program and after the program, but provides little information—unless interim measures are scheduled in the design—about what happened while the participant was in the program. Chen (1990) indicates that the simple input/output or pretest/posttest evaluation design "often will generate conclusions that are less than satisfactory" (p. 18).

These measures can be problematical with populations that have poor literacy skills. It is not safe to assume that respondents from such populations can read and understand the questions asked in paper-and-pencil measures.

■ Response Category Measures

Paper-and-pencil response-category measures seek short answers such as multiple-choice or true/false ratings. These instruments consist of various items intended to measure concepts such as self-esteem, achievement, depression, and the like. The operational definition is used to develop these items. Each item is designed to capture a particular facet of a complex concept because no single item is able to measure such a concept, for example, self-esteem, completely. Some items are made similar to one another so that evaluators can determine whether participants' responses are consistent. For example, on an achievement measure, if subtraction skills were being measured, several different subtraction problems, as well as several problems requiring the same kind of skill (e.g., borrowing), would be used to determine whether the respondent has truly mastered the skill of subtraction. Subtraction achievement would be measured by the number of correct responses for items that measure a specific skill.

Generally with paper-and-pencil measures, each item is accompanied by a list of categories represented by numbers. The respondent, or the person completing the measure, selects a number that "best represents" his or her answer. Common response categories include the following:

- Agreement categories (strongly disagree–strongly agree)
- Frequency categories (never–always)
- True/false

During analysis, all the responses to the items that measure an outcome are pooled together to determine the score. This score is usually compared with criteria used to rank the respondent. Such measures are commonly taken during the assessment or screening phase.

■ Standardized Measures

Many paper-and-pencil measures are standardized. This means that the measure is administered to the respondent and scored and the results are interpreted according to specific guidelines or directions that apply to every person completing the measure. In most cases, program evaluators should consider initially using, whenever possible, a standardized instrument to measure outcomes.

In general, a standardized instrument provides greater credibility for results because such measures or instruments have been tested and corrected for problems that almost always occur when "home-made" instruments are used. A manual provides information and instructions regarding the purpose and use of the instrument. Standardized instruments always report the following information.

- Operational definition
- Validity
- Reliability
- Appropriate populations

This information should always be reviewed before using the instrument as a measure to determine whether the instrument matches the program's outcomes and definitions. It is important to remember that program designers select the instrument that best measures the outcomes. In other words, programs are developed before the instrument is selected and are not built around a measure.

Operational Definition

Each standardized instrument that is selected as a measure of an outcome operationally defines that which is being measured. For example, Battle (1992), in the *Culture-Free Self-Esteem Inventories*, provides several definitions of self-esteem for children: general self-esteem, social self-esteem, academic self-esteem, and parent-related self-esteem. Each of these self-esteems has a separate definition because the inventory measures several different types of self-esteem. Each definition is based on the way the author of the inventory or instrument perceives each of these possible self-esteems. For example, Battle's operational definition of social self-esteem is "the aspect of self-esteem that refers to individuals' perceptions of the quality of their relationships with peers" (p. 3). If a program is intended to measure social self-esteem, this definition would be considered with regard to how well it reflects the operational definition of the program. If the two definitions did not match, the measure would be considered inappropriate.

Validity

Measures are valid if they measure what they intend to measure. In general, a measure is valid if it is agreed upon by several experts in the field, compares favorably to other measures that examine the same concept, and contains several items that consistently measure a particular concept (Rossi & Freeman, 1993).

A ruler is an example of a valid measuring tool. On some rulers, one side measures inches and the other side centimeters. If one wanted to measure the distance between points A and B in inches, the desired results would be a measure of inches—a valid result in that inches was predetermined to be the measure of choice. Using the centimeter side would produce results that are invalid because the results would not accurately reflect the distance in inches—the desired measure.

In a standardized measure, each operational definition and the corresponding items are thoroughly tested in several ways to ensure that that which is intended to be measured is measured. The results of a standardized instrument's extensive validity testing are reported in the administrator's manual.

Several types of validity checks may be discussed in the administration manual of a standardized instrument:

- *Face validity* describes how well the instrument measures what it says it will measure.
- *Content validity* describes how well and how accurately the instrument assesses the concepts being measured, usually in accordance with related research literature.
- *Concurrent validity* describes how well a measure correlates with another valid measure (Vogt, 1993).
- *Construct validity* describes how well each scale, dimension, concept outcome, etc., identified by the instrument is defined by the items that form a part of or make up the scale.

Descriptions of the various validity checks should be read carefully before using a standardized instrument.

Reliability

Reliability of the standardized instrument should also be considered before using it as a measure. Measures are considered reliable if they measure the same thing (the concept, the outcome) in the same way or produce the same results under the same conditions. In other words, in a repeated administration of the instrument, a measure can be relied upon to give the same or approximately the same results. Thus, reliable results are repeatable.

A scale is a good example of a reliable instrument. When several apples are weighed, the results might indicate that the apples weigh three pounds. To determine whether the scale is reliable, the apples are removed then weighed again on the same scale. If the apples are in the same condition during the second weighing as they were in the first weighing (no one, for example, has taken a bite of any of them) and they again weigh three pounds, then the scale can be considered to be reliable.

Similarly, with standardized instruments, if a program participant took a pretest more than once under the same conditions, then his or her score or results should be approximately the same on each measure. Program instruments must be known to be reliable at the outset because testing and retesting is not an efficient practice for any program. A reliable instrument assures program evaluators that the participants' scores would be repeated if the instrument were readministered.

Standardized measures are always tested for their reliability. Descriptions of how a measure's reliability was determined is found in the administrator's manual. This should be read carefully to understand the instrument's limitations in repeating a score.

Appropriate Populations

The appropriateness of an instrument for accurately measuring a program's participants also needs to be considered. This is essential in programs whose participants differ in some way from the general population. A description of the population used to test the instrument for its reliability is included in the administrator's manual. In reading these sections of the manual, evaluators should consider the groups used to test the instrument, the groups judged by the instrument authors to be appropriate for the instrument's use, and the groups for which the instrument is not appropriate. For example, Battle (1992) characterizes the Culture-Free Self-Esteem Inventory as "not recommended for children below Grade 2." Thus this instrument should not be used for children younger than six years of age.

The reading-skill level and vocabulary of the target population or populations for whom the instrument is intended must be considered when a test's examples, presentation, and format are being developed. The instrument should be tested on a population several times to determine its reliability in measuring the population. Changes may be made in the instrument to obtain the most valid and reliable measure from the target population.

Using an instrument on a population different from the one for which it is intended produces questionable results. The untested population may interpret the items differently from the instrument's target population and thereby give different responses. The responses of the two populations cannot be interpreted according to the same guidelines.

■ Types of Standardized Measures

Standardized measures are either norm referenced or criterion referenced. The difference between the two measures lies in how their scores are interpreted. In selecting either type of measure, evaluators should review the instrument manual carefully (Rossi & Freeman, 1993; Sax, 1974; Scriven, 1991).

Norm-Referenced Measures

Norm-referenced measures allow the target population's score to be compared with the score of a reference group. The target population's score is interpreted in relation to the reference group's score. A norm-referenced measure determines a given score's ranking in a range of scores within the reference group.

Usually, the actual score, or raw score, is converted to another score called a standard score. Several types of standard scores are commonly used by a norm-referenced test. The z-score, for example, uses 0 as the mean and a standard deviation of 1. The z-score is the most commonly used standard score (Vogt, 1993). The T-score uses a mean of 50 and a standard deviation of 10.

Percentile is a score of rank. A score at the 63rd percentile, for example, indicates that this score exceeds 63% of the total scores. Percentiles are based on rank order and therefore have no mean or standard deviation.

Normal curve equivalency (NCE) uses percentiles as scores. It has a mean of 50 and a standard deviation of 21.06. Scores are matched to the percentile ranks. For example, if a score is at the 35th percentile, the NCE is 35.

Criterion-Referenced Measures

Criterion-referenced measures determine a score and compare it with a predetermined expectation of what should be achieved. Criterion-referenced measures indicate what a participant should score in order to be considered as being at a particular level. Each level's criteria are clearly defined by the possible scores or the participant's performance on the measure.

■ Selecting a Standardized Instrument

Several factors should be considered in selecting a measure for program evaluation (Sax, 1974):

- *Cost* includes the purchase of the instrument, the answer sheets, and the scoring of the instrument if performed by outside experts or requires special expertise/training to score the answers.
- *Time* needed to administer the instrument, how administration of the instrument fits into the program activities, and how long it takes the participant to complete the instrument should be considered.
- *Administration, scoring, and interpretation* may be easy or may require special training.
- *Format* should be user friendly, provide good directions, present multiple-choice answers that make sense as possible answers, use appropriate vocabulary, and present a pleasing, attractive appearance. Care should be taken to ensure that participants do not feel overwhelmed by the test.
- *Different forms* may be necessary for the posttest, especially if the course of the program is brief and the person completing the measure is likely to remember items from the pretest.
- *Language alternatives* are necessary in programs that serve populations whose primary language is not English. Translations should be examined closely to make sure they correspond with the original version.
- *Multiple levels* of a measure allow the evaluator to compare pre- and posttest scores over periods during which it is expected that participants will change regardless of their participation in the program. For example, programs that serve the develolpmental needs of young children will want to measure gains in development. It

can be assumed that children will develop regardless of their participation in the program. Thus, the program must use a measure that accounts for developmental changes *and* measures individual growth resulting from program participation.

■ Selected References on Tests and Measures

Many reference resources are available at a local or university library to help locate standardized measures. Testing services provide catalogs with complete descriptions of various measures. These services send to their customers annual catalogs presenting new and revised measures as well as existing measures. A telephone representative can help locate a measure or describe a measure in greater detail.

■ Qualitative Measures

Qualitative measures provide information on the program's overall impact on outcomes as well as on the process of change. Miles and Huberman (1984) state, "Qualitative data . . . are a source of well-grounded, rich descriptions and explanations of processes occurring in local contexts" (p. 15).

Qualitative evaluation methods have various names, including naturalistic, phenomenological, and flexible, among others (Anastas & MacDonald, 1994; Lincoln & Guba, 1985). Evaluations that use qualitative methods describe the perceptions, experiences, and impact of the program on its participants, staff, and other important groups. Information is obtained through interviews, open-ended questions, review of documents and journals, observations, and so forth. Data collection is flexible, allowing for important information that had not been considered to emerge. Qualitative measures can produce unexpected results useful in revising or enriching a program. Qualitative results shine light on what happens in the "black box" of pretest/posttest evaluation designs.

Qualitative measures determine how well a program is doing with its participants when no standarized measures are available to assess program outcomes. Results from qualitative measures (such as interviews, focus groups, observations), when used with quantitative measures developed in-house and/or from background information of participants (demographic, attendance, etc.) can highlight the program's success in meeting its goals with current participants.

Qualitative measures have disadvantages as well. In particular, most stakeholders want numerical proof of a program's success. Most outside funders consider a numerical comparison to a norm or to criteria as concrete evidence of a program's success. Qualitative measures, as well as in-house quantitative measures, are not generalizable to the target population, and their reliability and validity are often questioned.

Another disadvantage is the amount of time required to complete qualitative measures. The depth and scope of qualitative information make it difficult to relate such information in directly measurable terms. Capturing and interpreting each participant's perceptions require a lot of staff, participant, and program-operation time.

The interview is the most common method used in qualitative measurements. Staff generally compose various questions asking participants for detailed descriptions of various aspects of their program experience. The interview in an outcome evaluation would focus on the expected outcome. Program participants might be asked to respond to the following:

- How did the participant feel before the program?
- What changes did the participant notice as a result of participation in the program?
- When did the participant notice the change?
- How does the participant feel about the change?
- What in the program helped the participant to make this change?
- What outside the program helped the participant to make the change?

As indicated, these questions do not ask for yes or no re-sponses; rather they explore with the participant the relationship between change and the program.

In designing qualitative evaluation methods, evaluators may conduct a brief interview with the participant before he or she begins the program (pretest) to determine what the participant expects to achieve, followed by another interview at the end of the program (posttest) to determine if the participant has achieved his or her goal and how it was accomplished. If an interview is done at the end of the program only, the participant is asked to reflect on his or her progress, achievements, and so forth.

Analyzing qualitative responses requires a lot of time. Responses are reviewed for common themes and trends, then crossed with other responses. To ensure that the interpretation is correct, two or more staff members independently interpret responses, then compare their interpretations for consistency. Results are summarized in a narrative format.

Qualitative measures are worth the time and effort. They can enhance and support outcome evaluation results.

■ Example Program Measures

The four examples' measures might be described as follows:

Example 1: *Parenting program.* The quantitative measure includes a standardized measure of the parenting skills taught in the program. The qualitative measure asks participants to describe how the program has helped them become better parents, what they continue to have difficulties with, and what they have learned in the program that they now use at home with their children.

Example 2: *Students at risk of dropping out of school.* The quantitative measure is determined by attendance records. The qualitative measure includes questions about working with the counselors, what motivates students to come to school, and what motivates students to skip school.

Example 3: *Job seekers.* The quantitative measure is a checklist of job skills and/or careers for which the participant is qualified. The qualitative measure includes questions about participants' knowledge of other jobs and job information they have received outside the program.

Example 4: *Independent living.* The quantitative measure is a depression checklist completed by a staff member. The qualitative measure asks participants their thoughts about their progress, their feelings about living independently, and what they need to continue to live independently.

■ Summary

Measuring tools to evaluate program outcomes must be selected carefully. It is important to look at each measure selected to determine its appropriateness to the program. Quantitative measures that do not reflect the program's purpose will produce results that cannot be interpreted. The program's operational definitions of expected outcomes guide the selection of measures.

Qualitative measures, although open-ended, should focus on the outcomes and be kept to manageable proportions. If a program uses qualitative measures, it must be prepared to invest significant staff and participant time to the collection and analysis of data.

To Do

1. Review operational definitions.
2. Determine if a norm-referenced or criterion-referenced test is desired.
3. Select quantitative measures that match operational definitions.
4. Review each quantitative measure for validity, reliability, and match to the target population.
5. Consider whether the measure is practical.
6. Determine if a qualitative measure will be used in the program as part of the evaluation.
7. Develop a measure that is focused on the outcomes but allows for the participant to elaborate and expand on his or her experiences and change.

References

Anastas, J., & MacDonald, M. (1994). *Research design for social work and the human services.* New York: Lexington Books.

Battle, J. (1992). *Culture-free self-esteem inventories* (2nd ed.). Austin, TX: Pro-Ed.

Chen, H-T. (1990). *Theory-driven evaluations.* Newbury Park, CA: Sage Publications.

Lincoln, Y., & Guba E. (1985). *Naturalistic inquiry.* Newbury Park, CA: Sage Publications.

Miles, M., & Huberman, A. M. (1984). *Qualitative data analysis.* Newbury Park, CA: Sage Publications.

Rossi, P. H., & Freeman, H. E. (1993). *Evaluation: A systematic approach.* Newbury Park, CA: Sage Publications.

Sax, G. (1974). *Principles of educational measurement and evaluation.* Belmont, CA: Wadsworth.

Scriven, M. (1991). *Evaluation thesaurus* (4th ed.) Newbury Park, CA: Sage Publications.

Vogt, W. P. (1993). *Dictionary of statistics and methodology.* Newbury Park, CA: Sage Publications.

6

Data Collection and Management

Key Terms

Data collection: The manner in which individual pieces of information are gathered from each participant.

Data management: The activities of compiling information into files for analysis.

Data set: A computer file that arranges information by rows and columns, wherein a row represents all the information from a single participant and a column a single piece of information from all the participants.

Variable: A column of numbers or values representing a single piece of information from all the participants in a data set. Variables are of four types: nominal, ordinal, interval, and ratio.

■ Introduction

Data collection and management in the evaluation design describe the process of gathering and structuring information for analysis. Only the data collected are the data analyzed. Although this fact may seem obvious, it is a serious consideration because the information collected and the form in which it is collected determine the types of analysis that can be done, which, in turn, affects the results obtained and the presentation of the final report.

After the evaluation has been developed—scheduling data collection, selecting data to be examined and analyzed, and selecting the instrument to measure outcomes—the data are then collected and organized into a data set. This data set must be structured in such a way that the data can be analyzed.

The first step of data collection, in most cases, is performed by all staff members as they enroll and assess participants and monitor their performance. This is especially true if the instruments used to collect information on outcomes are also part of the program's operational procedures. Because it is likely that more than one staff person will be involved in gathering information from the participant, data collection on the next level—moving the information from the data collectors to the data manager—must be an efficient system. The data manager is responsible for developing and monitoring the system and building the data set for analysis. In some cases this person also analyzes the data. The system for moving the data should include the following:

- Collect the data from each participant
- Build the data set
- Clean the data set
- Identify the variable types for analysis

This chapter reviews each of these parts of the data collection system. Although the system can be organized manually, our discussion in this chapter is based on building a data set in a computer and using a software package to analyze data.

Collecting Data

Moving the data from different locations, such as staff records and participant files, to the data manager requires specific tasks. Tasks can be a complex operation in that data may be located in many different places and handled by various staff. In other words, data collection can be time consuming. The data manager must be knowledgeable about where the various data on participants are located and which staff members have responsibility for maintaining the information in the sources or records. The data manager must develop a system that specifies which staff members should report the information required for the evaluation. This may be facilitated with a form that garners specific information on individual participants. To develop this form, the data manager should review the evaluation design and objectives to determine the data needed to satisfy the demands of the evaluation. For example, the parent-training program (example 1) requires information on the following:

- Parenting practices test scores or pre- and posttests (measures of the outcome)
- Parenting household status (two parent, single parent)
- Participant attendance to determine eligibility within the evaluation study

Using these guidelines, a data manager might develop the following form:

Parent Training Data Collection Form

1. Name of participant: _____

2. Participant's organization identification number: _____

3. Current parent household status (check one):
   ___ Single-parent household
   ___ Two-parent household
   ___ Other   Explain _____
   ___ Not reported/available

4. Parenting skills assessment pretest score: _____

5. Parenting skills assessment posttest score: _____

6. Number of sessions attended: _____

7. Comments: _____
_____

8. Completed by (name of staff member) _____

This data-collection form captures all the information needed for the evaluation design of the parenting program. Basic information is gathered and reported. If more information, such as age of participant, number of children in the family, and/or race/ethnicity, is desired, then these items would be added to the data-collection form. Note the comments section on the form. This item provides space for communicating with the data manager.

A staff member may have questions and information that he or she believes are relevant to the data being reported. Such information is usually important, and staff members completing the form should be encouraged to write any questions or comments they may have about the data they are reporting to the data manager.

Also reported on the form are the participant's name and organization identification number. Both of these pieces of information are important because they eliminate duplication of reported information. Errors in reporting information are minimized because name and identification number are used in cross-checking procedures.

Finally, the name of the staff person who completes or sends the report to the data manager is included on the form so the data manager has a contact person if confusing information needs clarification or confirmation.

The data manager should provide instructions for completing the form. Instructions should include the following:

- How to complete the form and what data sources to use
- Whom to contact regarding questions on how to complete the form
- Whom to return the form to and guidelines for sending the form
- Dates for returning the form

In collecting and moving data, it's necessary to take precautions to keep the information as confidential as possible. Because names and sensitive information on participants are matched on the data-collection forms, every effort should be made to maintain confidentiality throughout the data-collection and -manipulation process. Methods for securing a participant's confidentiality are generally developed according to agency procedures. Direct hand delivery in a sealed envelope is the simplest method. Information delivered over computer network systems requires an understanding of the networking system. It is important to evaluate networking systems to determine whether data should be sent through the system from staff person to data manager and whether this can be done without violating the confidentiality of the participant.

■ Building the Data Set

Data sets are built by the data manager. A data set is developed by using the data collection form and creating a codebook, the foundation of a data set. Data sets are built with a computer software package that has data-analysis capabilities.

A data set is also referred to as a data file. Almost all information in a data set is entered as a number. This means that all information that is not already in a number format must be changed into numbers. For example, the parent household status form has three options or categories for identifying the participant's parent household status. To make this information ready for a computer file, each of these options or categories must be assigned a number or code, for example, 1 for single-parent household, 2 for two-parent household, 3 for other types of households. These category codes would be entered into the computer data set as substitutes for the names of the categories. Other data, such as pre- and posttest scores, are already in a number format and can be entered into the computer data set.

A data file is organized in a row-by-column format. Each row of numbers represents all the information for each participant. Each column of numbers lists all participants' data for a single piece of information. Each column in a data set is referred to as a variable. These columns or variables are analyzed to obtain program results.

The codebook, a paper-and-pencil reference resource document, is the foundation on which a data set is built. It identifies the details of each variable. The codebook identifies the important information about each variable, such as the variable's name, computer name, range of numbers possible, where code numbers are assigned, what each of these codes represents, for example, in the household parenting status variable, and its column in the data set. Sometimes the original source of the data is included to facilitate answering questions on a participant's data. When new variables are added or changed in the data set, they are added to the codebook.

The following codebook (Figure 1) was developed from the parenting-practices program data-collection form. It is followed by the data set that would be created from the codebook's map. The codebook and the data set examples are described in reference to the codebook sections.

Sources

The *source* of the codebook indicates where the data, in their original form, come from. In the example data set, information was collected from three different sources: the intake form, test records, and attendance records. The source of the data is not entered into the data set.

Column and Width

The *column* of the codebook specifies in which column in the data set the variable will reside. For example, the variable ID (the participant's identification number) will reside in column 1, the variable *pretest* will reside in column 3, and so forth.

When building a data set, it's imperative to place comparable information from all participants in the appropriate variable columns. This ensures that the results will accurately reflect the

Figure 1. *Parenting Practices Program Codebook*

Source	Column	Width	Variable Name	Codes/ranges
Intake form	1	3	ID participant identification number	1–999
Intake form	2	1	PARENT participant's parent household status	1=single 2=two 3=other 9=missing/na
Test records	3	3	PRETEST pretest score	0–100 999=missing
Test records	4	3	POSTTEST posttest score	0–100 999=missing
Attendance records	5	2	ATTEND participant attendance record for 10 sessions	1–10 99=missing

Parenting Practices Data Set

Column 1 ID	Column 2 PARENT	Column 3 PRETEST	Column 4 POSTTEST	Column 5 ATTEND
001	1	19	48	10
002	2	38	54	10
003	9	31	32	7
004	3	30	29	9
005	2	30	81	7

information that is being examined. All of the participant ID numbers are listed in column 1 of the data set; all of the codes for the parent variable are listed in column 2 of the data set.

Depending on the computer software chosen to build the data set, the columns designated in the codebook may vary. In older versions of data software packages, the number of columns needed per variable is dependent upon the number of digits in the variable. For example, in the variable ID, it's possible to have identification numbers 100 or greater. Thus the identification number is three digits wide and requires three columns to list the variable. The width noted in the codebook indicates how many columns are needed for each variable.

In newer versions of data analysis software packages, a variable can have as many as eight digits per column. In Figure 1, the first variable, ID, is three digits wide, but because this example assumes a newer data software package, all three digits of the variable reside in column 1 of the data set.

The codebook should specify the columns, whether the number of columns equals the number of possible digits for each variable (for older software packages) or whether one column is associated with each variable (for newer software packages).

Variable Name

The variable name serves two functions in the codebook. First, it identifies the name that is used in the data set and, second, it specifies what the name represents. Computer software packages generally do not allow for lengthy variable names. In fact, eight characters (letters and numbers) are generally the maximum number of characters allowed in naming a variable. The characters that can be used often do not include spaces and other special symbols such as slashes, asterisks, question marks, and the like. Consequently, the data manager may become creative and somewhat abstract in developing variable names for the computer by dropping letters and pushing words together. Such abstract names can easily be forgotten over time. The codebook keeps track of these names by listing both the variable name and what it represents.

Codes/Ranges

Codes and *ranges* specify the possible numerical values entered into the data set. The information must be entered into the computer as numbers. If the information is not already in a number format, then numbers must be assigned to represent this information. In the variables in the example, codes or numbers were assigned to the categories within the variable. In the variable *ID*, each participant is considered his or her own category and therefore is assigned a number not greater than 999. For the variable, *parent*, 1 was assigned to represent single-parent households, 2 to represent two-parent households, and 3 to represent other types of households.

The range in the codebook represents the lowest and highest possible codes or number values for each variable. The range for *pretest* and *posttest* is 0 to 100, reflecting the lowest and highest possible scores on the parenting-assessment test.

For variables with categories, such as *parent,* the codes are defined. That is, 1 represents a single-parent household and is listed as "1 = single parent." Most software packages allow these category labels to be added to the variable so that the computer output can be read without referring to the codebook. It is always important to identify what a category represents.

Missing Data

Missing data are almost always encountered in data collection. Missing data are pieces of essential information that have not been collected from the participant or have not been properly recorded by participants or staff members. However, missing data should not be excessive for any given variable in a data set. If too many data are missing, then one should reexamine the procedures for collecting data.

Missing data cause problems in interpretation of results. For example, if half the participants who have completed the program do not take the final assessment, the results will represent only half of the participants and may or may not be representative of the entire program. If outcome data, such as scores on the pretest and posttest of the parenting program, are missing, it is almost impossible to capture the data. Missing pretests cannot be captured if the program participant has attended any of the program's sessions. Likewise, a missing posttest score is difficult to capture: If several weeks have passed since a participant left the program, other factors and influences may affect his or her posttest score. Program evaluations should attempt to maintain accurate representation of outcomes and other data.

Every effort to capture missing data should be made. This means time and leg work. One should never guess on missing data. Guessing distorts the evaluation results.

Missing data are entered into a data set with special codes. Each variable has a missing-data code, usually the last possible code in the range of possible codes. For example, the possible range for the variable parent is 1 to 9. The valid codes, as noted, are 1, 2, and 3, indicating the type of parenting household. For this variable, 9 is designated as the missing-data code. It would be used to identify participants who did not report or were not asked to report the type of parenting structure in the household. In the example, the participant with the ID number of 003 has a 9 entered in the parent variable column, indicating that the parenting structure for this participant is unknown.

After the data are entered into the data set, the final step is to instruct the computer how to read the numbers. Data analysis packages require that missing-data codes be identified by special commands when building the data set. This special command tells the software package that these values are not to be considered as a valid code or value and should be skipped in most analyses.

■ Cleaning the Data Set

After a data set has been built, errors must be eliminated. This task actually begins before data are entered by examining the data reporting forms and following up on missing data, inconsistent data, or confusing data. For example, a parent participant may have entered two categories for parenting household. Only one of the categories can be entered. Which one? Guesses are not allowed, so follow-up is necessary. Or perhaps the pretest score is higher than the posttest score. Although this is within the realm of possibility, one should confirm that the participant did indeed lose ground after participating in the program.

After data are entered into the computer, another cleaning check is made. Checking the data entered is a good idea in order to be certain that data are being correctly entered. This task may be time consuming, but it helps avoid costly errors down the road.

■ Variable Identification

Identifying types of variables in the data set provides guidance for the kinds of analysis that can be done. Each variable in the data set falls into one of four variable types:

- ■ Nominal variables
- ■ Ordinal variables
- ■ Interval variables
- ■ Ratio variables

Variables are typed according to the type of information or data contained in them. The numbers in a variable measure some concept. How these numbers are defined and how the numbers relate to one another determine the variable type.

Nominal Variables

Nominal variables are the simplest of the variable types. The numbers of a nominal variable represent categories, groups, or specific characteristics. For example, in the parent variable, three categories were noted: single parent, two parent, and other. In the codebook, numbers were assigned to represent each of these three categories: 1 for single parent, 2 for two parent, and 3 for other.

The numbers in a nominal variable do not have any relationship to one another. They are used simply as symbols of the category. Any three numbers could have been used to represent the categories in this variable because number assignment to categories in a nominal variable is an arbitrary decision. The numbers do not have any rank order. A given number is not higher or lower, better or worse, more or less than the other numbers. In the parent variable, no judgments are made about the number of parents in the household. The number merely identifies each participant's parenting household status.

ID is the other nominal variable used as an example in this chapter. Each participant had his or her own category within the variable ID. An identification number in this variable simply identifies the participant's row of data in the data set. It is not used to rank or form judgments about participants.

Ordinal Variables

Numbers in an ordinal variable are rank ordered. Ordinal variables are commonly used on surveys that use rating scales to capture respondents' opinions, perceptions, and so forth. For example, a perception-of-satisfaction rating might use a scale of 1 to 6 in which 1 represents very dissatisfied and 6 represents very satisfied.

In a rating scale from 1 to 6, the actual distance between 1 and 2, 2 and 3, 3 and 4, 4 and 5, and 5 and 6 is not known. For example if a person completing a survey chooses a 2 on a rating scale, it is not known whether the 2 represents a value a lot higher than a 1 rating and is close to, but not quite, a 3. Another person's rating might fall closer to the 1 rating, but the evaluation has no way of knowing. In other words, both persons' 2 rating may relate differently to the 1 and 3 ratings. The evaluator, however, can only rank the order, not the degree of the rating.

Interval Variables

Numbers in an interval variable are also rank ordered, as in the ordinal variables, but the exact distance between any two numbers is known and is consistent with the distance of any other two numbers similar in order. For example, if number of pounds is used as the unit of measure to determine weight, one knows that the difference between 2 and 3 pounds is exactly the same as the difference between 38 and 39 pounds. The difference, or the unit of measure, is the interval.

In the parenting program, one interval variable—attend—was used. The unit of measure between any two given measures is one program session.

Ratio Variables

The numbers in a ratio variable are treated the same way as interval variables are treated. The only difference between an interval variable and ratio variable is that a ratio variable has an absolute zero and an interval variable does not. In the parenting program, pretest and posttest variables both have an absolute zero, because it is possible to have no correct answers. This is known because the range of possible scores listed in the codebook is 0–100.

Variables can be simple or complex, depending how the numbers are treated. More complex variables can be changed or considered as a lower-order variable type, but the reverse is not true. In other words, nominal variables can never be considered anything other than nominal variables. Ordinal variables can be considered nominal variables, but not interval or ratio variables.

■ Summary

Data are collected on all participants in a program and sent to the data manager, who builds and cleans the data set. Data sets are described in a data codebook, which details all the information that will be stored in the data set. Codebooks are a reference document for the numbers and variables that serve as abbreviated representations of longer and more complex concepts.

As data sets are built, evaluators follow up on missing information in order to obtain the most complete data set possible. Each line of data is reviewed for errors in entering data, inconsistent reporting, and confusion.

Finally, variables are identified according to their type: nominal, ordinal, interval, or ratio. Recognizing each variable's type provides guidance in the kinds of data analysis that can be done on the variable.

To Do

1. Set data collection time line based on evaluation design.

2. Develop a data collection form that reports each participant's demographic, outcome, and other information relevant to the study.

3. Train staff in procedures for reporting data to the data manager.

4. Develop a codebook and build a data set.

5. Follow up on all missing data.

6. Clean data set.

7. Identify variable types.

7

Data Analysis

Key Terms

Distributions: Analysis showing how the values in a given variable are spread from lowest to highest. Distributions are of two types: (1) frequency or counts of participants at each value and (2) percent or proportion of participants at each value.

Measure of central tendency: Analysis showing where the average or center value is located in a variable. Central tendency measures are of three types: mode, median, and mean.

Measure of dispersion: Analysis of how far apart or close together values are within a variable. Dispersion may be one of three types: index of dispersion, range, and standard deviation.

■ Introduction

Quantitative data analysis requires knowledge in two areas: variable types (discussed in chapter 6) and types of statistics. Variables can be one of four types, each of which has restrictions on the type of statistical analysis that can be applied. This is so even with basic descriptive statistics related to a single variable.

Statistics software does *not* distinguish among variable types. Statistical analysis packages compute the analysis as requested on any type of variable, but the results may be difficult to interpret and, in some cases, make no sense at all. It is the responsibility of the person analyzing the data to know the types of variables and select the most appropriate analysis. Various types of statistics range from the very basic, using one variable, called univariate or descriptive statistics, to analysis using many variables of different types, called multivariate statistics.

The purpose of this chapter is to introduce basic descriptive statistics related to a single variable, or univariate statistics. The following concepts are reviewed: distributions, both frequency and percent; measures of central tendencies, mode, median, and mean; measures of dispersion, index of dispension, range, and standard deviation; and change scores. Regardless of the complexity of the analysis undertaken, all analysis plans begin with univariate statistics.

■ Distributions

Distribution in univariate analysis is a picture of how the numbers within a variable are spread across the possible range of a variable. It is an initial picture of what the data on a given variable look like as a whole. This picture provides necessary information used to identify whether follow up is needed because of missing data as well as to help interpret other analyses such as averages and variability. Distributions are of two types: frequency and percent.

Frequency Distributions

A frequency distribution is an actual count of the number of participants at each value or category code that has been entered into the variable being analyzed. It lists all the values or codes, beginning with the lowest value or code and following a sequential order to the highest value or code. All values that have been entered into the data set are listed.

Next to each value listed, the number (reported as *n*) of participants who have had the value entered into their row of data in the data set are counted. In addition to counting participants with valid values or codes, frequency distributions also report the number of participants with missing data. This means that a frequency distribution can have two totals: a total of all the participants with valid values or codes and a total of all the participants with valid and missing values and codes. The latter total should be the same as the total number of participants entered into the data set. The former total excludes missing data and equals the total number of participants only if no data are missing in the variable being analyzed. Large amounts of missing data present problems in data analyses and interpretation of results.

Cumulative frequency distribution, or valid cumulative frequency distribution, is another type of distribution. It begins with the lowest value, totals the frequency of it and the next value, and adds the frequency of each subsequent value. Cumulative frequency indicates at any given point on the distribution how many participants scored at that value and below. At the final value, the cumulative frequency will total the number of participants who have valid codes or values. In addition to providing a numerical picture of the distribution, the number cumulative frequency is helpful in finding percents and measures of central tendency.

Percent Distributions

Percent distributions are distributions of proportions. They are also referred to as relative frequencies and are generally included with a frequency distribution. Percent distributions are of three types: percent, valid percent, and cumulative percent. All percents are calculated by dividing the number or frequency of participants at a given value by the total number of participants.

The difference between a *percent* and a *valid percent* distribution lies in the choice of total *N* used. The percent distribution includes the total number of participants in the data set, which includes the missing data values. A valid percent distribution excludes participants who are coded as having missing data in the variable under consideration and is reflected in the cumulative frequency distribution.

A cumulative percent distribution totals the percents of each of the values or categories on the valid percent distribution. A cumulative percent distribution begins with the lowest value's calculated percent, then adds the next value's percent to it. The total cumulative percent equals 100%.

The following example illustrates frequency and percent distributions with the parenting program data. Two variables are used to illustrate results: *parent*, a nominal variable, and *pretest*, an interval variable. A total of 38 persons participated in this evaluation study.

Example 1—*Parent:* The variable *parent* is nominal and has three valid categories (see codebook in chapter 6). The categories are not rank ordered and are as follows:

  1 = single-parent household
  2 = two-parent household
  3 = other type of household
  9 = missing

Table 4 shows the distribution results of this variable. The parenting program served a total of 38 participants; the frequency distribution indicates that 21 participants were single parents. By means of the percent column, it can be seen that proportionately 55.3% of the participants had a single-parent household and 36.8% a two-parent household. The program also served two households,

Table 4. Distributions of Parenting Household Variable

Value/ category name	Value/ category code	Frequency	Cumulative frequency	Percent	Valid percent	Cumulative percent
Single	1	21	21	55.3	56.8	56.8
Two	2	14	35	36.8	37.8	94.6
Other	2	2	37	5.3	5.4	I00.0
Missing	9	1	missing	2.6	missing	
Total		38	37	100.0	100.0	

or 5.4% of the participants, categorized as other. One participant (2.6%) was categorized as having missing data on this variable.

The valid percents show a slight increase because the missing data are eliminated from the calculation. These parents were calculated on a total of 37 participants, because the data set had a missing data value or code on one participant. The cumulative percent shows the addition of the valid percent column from the lowest value or code to the highest value or code. When single- and two-parent households are added together, the result indicates that 94.6% ($n =$ 35) participated in the program. When the "other" category, with a 5.4% ($n = 2$), is added to the 94.6%, the cumulative percent is 100%.

Example 2—*Pretest:* This variable is an interval variable. Its values represent test scores on the pretest used to measure knowledge of parenting skills in the program. The values do not have names as the nominal variable values had in Example 1. See Table 5 for a distribution of the interval variable.

In the pretest variable, the percent distribution is the same as the valid percent distribution because no missing data were entered for any of the participants. All participants had, in fact, been pretested on the parenting-skills test.

This distribution shows that even though the test itself has a possible scoring range from 0 to 100 (see codebook in chapter 6), the actual scores of this group of participants ranged from 18, the lowest value scored on the pretest, to 40, the highest value scored on the pretest. It can be noted in the cumulative percent column that a little more than half of the participants (52.6%) scored fewer than 30 points on this pretest.

Table 5. *Distribution of Pretest Scores: An Interval Variable*

Value	Frequency	Cumulative frequency	Percent	Percent valid	Percent cumulative
18	2	2	5.3	5.3	5.3
19	3	5	7.9	7.9	13.2
21	1	6	2.6	2.6	15.8
22	4	10	10.5	10.5	26.3
24	1	11	2.6	2.6	28.9
25	1	12	2.6	2.6	31.6
27	3	15	7.9	7.9	39.5
28	3	18	7.9	7.9	47.4
29	2	20	5.3	5.3	52.6
30	6	26	15.8	15.8	68.4
31	2	28	5.3	5.3	73.7
32	3	31	7.9	7.9	81.6
33	2	33	5.3	5.3	86.8
34	1	34	2.6	2.6	89.5
36	1	35	2.6	2.6	92.1
38	1	36	2.6	2.6	94.7
39	1	37	2.6	2.6	97.4
40	1	38	2.6	2.6	100.0
Total	38		100.0	100.0	

Other information can be obtained or viewed in a different light from the cumulative percent column. Instead of noting that a little more than half scored fewer than 30 points, another view of the results shows that more than two-thirds (68.4%) of the participants scored 30 points or fewer on the pretest.

Distributions on interval variables show how the scores are spread, where the center is likely to be, and how far apart the scores are from one another. Distributions are closely linked to measures of central tendency and measures of variability.

■ Measures of Central Tendency

Measures of central tendency look at the center value of the distribution of the valid values or scores. Missing data are excluded in calculating these measures. Central tendency measures are of three kinds, all of which are commonly referred to as "average"—mode, median and mean. Of these three, the most widely known is the mean, the only one of the three averages of central tendency measures that uses arithmetic to find the center. These averages and their corresponding measures of variability are versatile and useful for gaining insight into program performance.

Mode

Mode is the most frequently occurring category or value in a given variable. It is easily found in a frequency or percent distribution by looking for the category or value with the highest number or percent of participants. In the parent variable, the mode is category 1 or single parent. This category has the highest number of participants ($n = 21$) and the highest percent of participants (56.8%).

In the pretest variable, the mode is the value 30 because the number of participants scoring 30 points on the pretest is greater than any other value of the variable. Six participants in this variable scored 30 points, accounting for 15.8% of the participants.

A variable can have more than one mode if two or more categories or values are equal in frequency and percent and are higher than any other category or value.

Modes may be reported for all types of variables and are useful in interpreting the other averages—median and mean. Mode is most often reported for nominal variable or variables with categories.

Median

The median indicates the exact center of all values or codes. It is most frequently used for variables such as ordinal, interval, and ratio.

To find the median, all scores in a variable are rank ordered. The number of rank-ordered values listed should equal the number of participants with valid values (missing data are excluded). The median is the exact middle score; it can be the same as values before and after it or it can be a value that is not listed. For example, in instances in which the scores are even in number and a gap exists between the top half and bottom half, the median is the middle value within this gap. Therefore, the median may not even be listed

Table 6. Distribution List to Find the Median
18
18
19
19
19
21
22
22
22
22
24
25
27
27
27
28
28
28
29
Median
29
30
30
30
30
30
30
31
31
32
32
32
33
33
34
36
38
39
40

in the valid values that are rank ordered. This "gap" may be any size. For example, if the top score of the bottom half of the rank order is 5.0 and the bottom score of the top half is 5.5, the median score is 5.25.

The median is not affected by extreme scores in the list of values. The median is always the exact middle value when the list of values is divided in half.

Table 6 lists values from the pretest variable, showing 38 valid values. The median in this list is 29 because 19 scores are above the median and 19 scores are below the median. The highest value of the lower half of the list is 29 and the lowest value of the upper half of the list is 29. The middle of the two numbers 29 and 29 is 29. Therefore, the median in the pretest variable is 29. Had the middle of the list fallen between 29 and 30, the median would have been 29.5—the exact middle.

Mean

Means are most widely used in statistics. To find the mean, one needs simple arithmetic skills. It is calculated by dividing the sum of the valid values by the total number of valid values. Missing data are excluded from this calculation. The mean is calculated on interval and ratio variables. The steps for finding the mean are as follows:

- Add all the valid values to be considered in the mean.
- Divide the sum by the total number of valid scores.
- Result is the mean.
    1. $1 + 2 + 3 + 5 + 9 = 20$
    2. $20 / 5 = 4$
    3. mean (or M) = 4

Means are sensitive to extreme values, that is, those values that are much higher or lower than the other values in the distribution, because such values distort the mean. For example, if five people take a test, the scores of which may range from 0 to 100, and score 7, 9, 10, 14, and 95, the 95 score will distort the mean because it is so much higher than the others. In this scenario, the mean equals 27, a score that is much higher than the scores of four of the five scores. Thus critical errors can be made in interpreting the meaning of test results if one considers the mean only. In fact, the median value for these scores is only 10.

A single extreme score is very easy to spot in a frequency distribution. However, extreme scores are not so easily noticed in large data sets in which several high (or low) scores occur in a wide distribution. A simple way to check for the mean's sensitivity or pull in a positive or negative direction is to compare it with the median. Because the median and the mean represent the center and average values, respectively, ideally they should be approximately equal. If these two measures of central tendency diverge widely, then the mean is distorted. In such cases, one should give more weight to the median score. In the parent program example, the variable pretest mean is 28 and the median is 29. Thus the mean and median support each other.

■ Measures of Dispersion

Measures of dispersion analyze the distance and closeness of values. The three measures of dispersion are often referred to as measures of variability:

- Index of dispersion
- Range
- Variance/standard deviation

Measures of dispersion are usually reported with measures of central tendency to provide a more complete picture of the values in a variable.

Index of Dispersion

The index of dispersion is used to look at the mode and therefore is best used with nominal variables. The index of dispersion is the *total percent of all the nonmodal categories* and may be calculated by subtracting the percent of the modal category from 100% (Anastas & MacDonald, 1994). The index of dispersion provides perspective on the modal category's majority. The nominal variable of religion in Table 7 has six valid categories. The percent distribution indicates that 40.5% are Christian; this is the mode. The index of dispersion

Table 7. Example of Index of Dispersion

Religion	Valid percent
Buddhist	8.1%
Christian	40.5%
Jewish	27.0%
Muslims	16.2%
No preference	5.2%
Other	3.0%

shows that the total of all other categories is 59.5%, suggesting great diversity within this variable of religious preference.

In the parent variable in example 1, the modal category is single-parent household, with 56.8% of the participants identified as single parents. All other categories represent 43.2% of the program.

Range

The range identifies the highest and lowest values. It is reported with the median and mean and therefore is used with any rank-ordered variables—ordinal, interval, or ratio. It can be reported in two ways:

- Simply identify the highest and lowest valid values within the variable.
- Subtract the lowest valid value from the highest valid value.

In the pretest variable of Example 2, the range may be reported as follows

- Minimum value = 18; maximum value = 40
- Range = 22

The range considers the valid scores in the variable, not the possible range of valid scores as reported in the codebook.

Variance/Standard Deviation

Variance and standard deviation are different sides of the same coin. Standard deviation is the square root of variance and is the measure of dispersion that is usually reported. This measure evaluates the distance, on average, among variables. Large standard deviations indicate that values are far apart from one another, whereas small standard deviations indicate that the values are very close together. Standard deviation is appropriately reported for the mean and is used on interval or ratio variables. Calculating a standard deviation can be done by hand on a calculator with a square root function. Generally, though, statistical software packages calculate the standard deviation when the mean is calculated. Using a hand calculator, the calculation steps are as follows:

- Find the mean of the variable.
- From each valid value, subtract the mean.
- Square each of the resulting values to eliminate all negative numbers.
- Total all the squared values.
- Divide by the total number of values.
- Find the square root of the result.

With this procedure the average of the distances from the mean is calculated. In step one the mean of the variable has to be calculated to begin the process of finding the average distance from the mean. Step two uses the mean to determine the difference or actual distance each value is from the mean. Remember, the mean is a measure of central tendency; it is the center of the variable. Thus, the further away a value is from the mean, the bigger the difference. All values that are lower than the mean will result in negative differences. All values higher than the mean will result in positive differences.

Because the standard deviation looks for the average of the distances from the mean, the column of negative and positive differences cannot be used because the sum would be zero. The negative differences below the mean will cancel the positive differences above the mean. In order to avoid this problem, all the differences, both negative and positive, are squared or multiplied individually. A negative multiplied by a negative produces a positive number, just as a positive multiplied by a positive produces a positive number.

After all the differences are squared, the mean or average distances can be calculated by adding all the squared numbers and dividing by the total number of values—steps four and five. The result is the variance of the variable. To find the standard deviation (step six) the square root is calculated. At this juncture, finding the square root undoes the squaring of each value performed in step three. The standard deviation is the mean or average distance of any given value in a variable from the central tendency—the mean. See Figure 2 for an example of this calculation.

Figure 2. Calculating Standard Deviation

Step 1:	Step 2:	Step 3:	Step 4: Total of Step 3 = 120
Values			
10	10–15 = –5	25	
10	10–15 = –5	25	Step 5: Divide total
12	12–15 = –3	9	by N = 120/10 = 12
14	14–15 = –1	1	
16	16–15 = 1	1	Step 6: Find the
16	16–15 = 1	1	square route: 3.46.
16	16–15 = 1	1	
17	17–15 = 2	4	The standard
17	17–15 = 2	4	deviation of this
22	22–15 = 7	49	list of values is 3.46.
The mean of these values = 15			

■ Change Scores

Change scores are the calculated difference between the posttest and the pretest. This calculation is used to determine how much change has occurred in each participant from beginning the program to exiting the program. Change scores are calculated first on each individual participant's pre- and posttest scores. Then the appropriate measures of central tendency and dispersion are calculated. Change scores are *not* determined by subtracting the pretest mean from the posttest mean.

After pretest scores and posttest scores are entered, the statistical software package should be capable of doing the appropriate subtraction and creating a new variable in the process. This new variable is the change score or the difference between the pre- and posttest results. This new variable should be saved into the data set and noted in the codebook.

After this procedure is completed, descriptive analysis can be done on the variable. A frequency distribution is helpful in identifying negative change scores—participants who scored lower on the posttest than on the pretest. The distribution is helpful in finding the percent of participants who scored above the standard.

■ Summary

This chapter presents analysis techniques necessary for completing a basic program evaluation describing outcome results. The three analyses presented—distributions, central tendencies, and dispersions—are used specifically with particular variable types and are useful when used in concert for presenting data as well as verifying results. Frequency distributions help validate the standard deviation, and means are checked against the medians to determine whether extreme scores have occurred. (Computer packages frequently have the capacity to perform more basic analysis than is presented in this chapter. Review the computer software material to determine its capabilities.)

After data results are generated, new questions can be asked or the same questions asked but in a different way. For example, the outcomes of single parents may be examined separately in order to determine how this group is doing in the program. The questions are easily answered by the computer software package, which can sort out a variable's categories and analyze the outcomes separately by each category.

Data can be looked at and explored in various ways, even when one uses basic descriptive analyses. However, analyses must be planned in advance of data collection. Knowing what is being looked at and how it will be measured determines the analysis plan.

To Do

1. Analyze data according to analysis plan.
2. Examine initial results for inconsistencies and follow up accordingly.
3. Determine the appropriate central tendency and dispersions measures for each variable.
4. Complete all analyses required for the report.

References

Anastas, J., & MacDonald, M. (1994). *Research design for social work and the human services.* New York: Lexington Books.

8

Reporting Evaluation Results

Key Terms

Evaluation report: Documentation of evaluation results, managed and written by program evaluator; product of staff or selected staff members.

Executive summary: Brief overview of the evaluation results.

■ Introduction

After the data analysis is completed, the report is prepared. The first step is to organize the results in a coherent way and report the results to staff or selected staff. This is the responsibility of the evaluator or manager of the evaluation. The immediate results are generated by the software program. These results are compiled in the order in which the analysis was completed.

Next, the results are given to staff to examine and interpret. In examining the results, additional questions may arise that are important in understanding the results; further analysis may be needed. Interpretation of the results is a staff responsibility, because they are familiar with the program. Staff members interpret the results by offering considerations, reasons, or possible explanations for the results. For example, a program may show poor attendance among participants. Staff members might explain this by noting that the program was held during a difficult winter during which many snow days made travel difficult for participants.

At this point, staff should not argue about whether the results are valid or reliable. Arguments regarding design, data collection, or other evaluation activities should not be part of the discussion on results interpretation. Interpretations of results are resolved and agreed upon before evaluation activities are initiated.

In general, arguments tend to arise when results are unexpected. Most staff members have preconceived notions of evaluation results. However, results generally provide some surprises— some pleasant and others not so pleasant. Because staff members are answerable to program results, it is important that they are not surprised when results are released to other stakeholder audiences. If staff members are informed of results before they are released officially, staff members have an opportunity to consider the implications of the results, formulate strategies for program operations, and respond to comments and criticisms of various stakeholder groups in a professional manner. It is not the responsibility of the evaluator to interpret results, but rather to lead staff through results interpretation.

The interpretation of results sessions should conclude with strategies and recommendations for program improvement, identification of program strengths, commendations, and program trends. This information is used to close the report and to provide direction for the following year's program evaluation.

Recommendations are developed on the basis of the results from the current evaluation and from prior evaluations. These recommendations are included in the next round of evaluation activities if the appropriate stakeholder groups (staff, administration, etc.) decide to act on them.

Prior years' recommendations that have been acted upon are also addressed in the current evaluation, assuming that these recommendations were part of the current year's evaluation study. Perhaps earlier recommendations stated a need to watch a particular trend or change.

Staff feedback and interpretation of results do not modify the results in any way. Results are fixed; they cannot change. They must be reported as they were analyzed in comparison with the program objectives. Decisions regarding the altering of data in any way, such as rounding off numbers to the nearest whole number or elimination of data on selected participants, must be reported.

Finally, all written reports should be reviewed for accuracy and consistency before being released to stakeholder groups. How and when each report is released to a stakeholder group is based on individual program needs and requirements.

■ Evaluation Report Contents

Regardless of the format and style, the level of specificity, the length of the evaluation report, and the stakeholder groups for whom it is written, all reports contain some common elements.

- Introduction
- Description of participants
- Methods used in the evaluation

- Program objectives and standards of success
- Results and interpretation
- Recommendations and commendations

Introduction to Report

The introduction of an evaluation report should include a brief overview of the program, its goals, and the purpose of the evaluation. The program philosophy and/or theoretical foundations may also be included in the introduction.

The introduction may also include recommendations from prior years' evaluations that have been addressed in the current evaluation. This signals to the reader that previous evaluation results and the recommendations that accompanied them have been considered and used for program maintenance and improvement.

Example 1: Introduction

This report presents the evaluation results of the Parenting Program for the 1995–1996 fiscal year. The goal of the program is to help parents of young children gain an awareness of effective parenting practices. In a small-group, classroom setting format for 10 sessions, parents hear lectures and participate in group discussions and activities designed to develop new or to enhance existing disciplinary skills that promote healthy child development and parent–child relationships. Five groups were conducted during the year with approximately eight parents per group.

This evaluation reports on the fifth year of the program's operation. In the past two years, the program has looked at the gains in parenting practice knowledge as based on the Parenting Practice Scale. Two recommendations were offered in the 1994–1995 evaluation and were included in this year's evaluation

- Look at the outcome by parenting status (single-parent, two-parent, other).
- Include a feedback session with the parents on the last day of program to gain insight into their reactions to the program and what they learned.

Description of the Participants

First, the target population is described. This description may include demographic information about program participants included in the study. A description of the groups within the target population is also provided. For example, in the parenting program, the single-parent household, two-parent household, and other types of household might be described. If this information has been maintained in the course of several evaluation studies, current demographics may be presented with past years' demographics. Statements about trends may be offered for consideration.

This section of the report may also include a description of participants who were in the program but not included in the study. Reasons for not including these participants should be stated. It may be important to keep "tabs" on these excluded participants because they may offer insight into trends and possible future directions of the program. Early detection of changes in the target population can be used to initiate program changes, revise recruitment practices, and support program expansion.

Finally, attendance results can be reported in this section. These results constitute a behavior of the participants rather than an outcome.

Example 1: Participants

The parenting program is targeted to any parent with a child six years old or younger. This year a total of 39 persons participated in the parenting program and all but one were included in the evaluation study. This exception was a day-care worker who was returning to a day-care-center job and who wanted to brush up on disciplinary skills.

This year, parents were asked to identify their parenting household status. Thirty-seven of the 38 participants did so. Parent households were as follows:

- 56.8% (n = 21) single-parent households
- 37.8% (n = 14) two-parent households
- 5.4% (n = 2) three-parent households (a grandparent lived with the family and was considered a parenting figure). Because this is the first year that this information was tallied, it cannot be compared with prior program years.

Attendance results showed that participants attended a mean of eight sessions. Less than a quarter of the participants attended all 10 sessions of the program. See Table 8 on page 96.

Table 8. Attendance of Participants

Number of sessions	n	%
7	9	23.7
8	12	31.6
9	8	21.1
10	9	23.0

Methods

The methods section of the evaluation report provides insight into the evaluation practices as well as allows for replication of the study in the future. This section includes descriptions of the design (pretest/posttest), operational definitions, instruments used to collect the data, and the procedures used to collect the data.

Example 1: Evaluation Methods

The outcome examined in this study was parenting techniques defined as identified effective methods of discipline as measured by the standardized instrument of Practices for Parenting Young Children [author's name and year of publication]. A paper-and-pencil assessment required 15 minutes to complete. The range of scores on this assessment is 0–100, with 100 being a perfect score.

Program participants were assessed for their current knowledge on the first day of the program and again on the last day of the program. Their gain in knowledge is considered representative of the program's outcome.

Participants were asked to participate in an end-of-session focus group. They were asked to relate their perceived gains in parenting knowledge and improvements they might suggest.

Program Objectives and Standards of Success

Each of the program objectives and the standards of success are restated to allow readers to place the results in context. Questions that were identified during the designing of the evaluation might also be included in this section.

Results and Interpretations

Results are reported by objective. The section noted above can be included with the results. In fact, it may be helpful to state the objective, report the results, and indicate whether the program met its standards for success before presenting other material. This keeps the focus of the report clean of other information such as trends and interpretations.

Interpretations of results are discussed separately from the results. Results are simple statements of facts, not interpretations of these facts. Results are viewed through the interpretive lens of staff and the evaluator. Mixing results with their interpretation can be confusing to the reader and may be viewed as an attempt to sway the opinions of stakeholder groups. If such perceptions are allowed to ferment, they may contaminate the accomplishments of the program in stakeholders' minds. It is important to keep this caveat in mind because evaluators tend to want to report more rather than less. A simple statement of the results and how these results compare with the standards of success is all that is necessary.

This section should be concluded by comparing this year's results with prior years' evaluation results. Again, the results should be presented before they are interpreted. This *trend analysis* leads into the final section of the report—recommendations and commendations.

Example 1: Objectives and Results
The objective and standard of success is as follows: When given a list of parenting practices, 70% or more participants will increase their pretest score by 20 or more points on taking a posttest.

Results show the mean change in scores among participants from pretest to posttest was an increase of 29.1 points on the Parenting Practice Scale. Table 9 below presents the results of this analysis.

Table 9. Participant Scores on Parenting Practice Scale

	N	Median	Mean	SD	Low Score	High Score
Pretest	38	29.0	28.0	5.9	18	40
Posttest	38	56.5	57.1	29.6	14	98
Change	38	30.0	29.1	29.9	−17	+77

These results show that upon entering the program, participants scored low on the scale, with an average of 28.0 points. The range on the pretest was also within 28 points, indicating that participants entered the program at about the same level of knowledge of parenting skills.

Posttest scores show a mean test score of 57.1 points, an average increase of 29.1 points. However, the range on the posttest score is much wider, with a spread of 84 points. The change-scores results show that some participants actually decreased their score.

Finally, results show that 60.5% of the participants increased their scores by 20 or more points. This does not meet the current objective's standard of success, whereby 70% or more of the participants would increase their score by 20 or more points.

Past Results

In the past two years, the program has shown similar gains in participant knowledge.

Year Average (mean)	Gains
1993–1994	35.3 points
1994–1995	27.3 points
1995–1996	29.1 points

Additional Results

Additional questions regarding the outcome were asked during the planning of the evaluation. These questions and results are listed below and are summarized in Table 10.

- **Question 1:** *Do single parents score 20 points or more on the posttest?* Results show that from the pretest to the posttest single parents' (n = 21) mean change in scores was an increase of 32.1 points. Approximately 66.6% (n = 14) of the single parents met the standard of success.
- **Question 2:** *Do partnered parents score 20 points or more on the posttest?* Results show that partnered parents from the pretest to the posttest (n = 14) had a mean increase in score of 31.1 points. Approximately 85.7% (n = 13) met the standard of success.
- **Question 3:** *Do other parenting households score 20 points or more on the posttest?* Results show that other households from the pretest to the posttest (n = 2) had a mean decrease in score of 3 points. Neither of these parents met the standard of success.

Table 10. Parenting Group Change–Score Results

	N	Median	Mean	SD	Minimum	Maximum
Single	21	40.0	32.1	33.1	−17	77
Partnered	14	33.0	31.1	25.0	− 5	71
Other	2	− 3.0	− 3.0	2.8	− 5	− 1

These results show that the program meets the standard of success with two-parent households but does not meet the standard of success with single parents or other parenting households (see Table 11).

Table 11. Percent of Parenting Groups Meeting Standard of Success Percent

	Percent
Single	66.6
Partnered	85.7
Other	0.0

Results of End-of-Program Focus Group

During a focus group, participants were asked to report any of their perceived gains in parenting knowledge and what improvements they might suggest. Results are as follows:

Gains in Parenting Knowledge

Parents reported that because of the program they knew more about:
- Child development and how a child thinks about the parent–child relationship
- Parenting and use of skills
- Other parents sharing the same concerns, making participants feel as though they are not "the only ones" when they feel unsuccessful in disciplining their child.

Program Improvement

Participants suggested the following:
- More participant sharing of the effectiveness of a new parenting practice
- More handouts that could be used between program ses-

sions as a guide for new techniques
- More emphasis on single parents' special needs for managing child behavior
- Shortening the number of sessions to eight by combining one or two topics.

Discussion of Results

The results of the parenting scale and the focus group show that the program needs to review its curriculum in terms of nontraditional parenting households. When combined, more than 61% of this year's participants were single parents or maintained other parenting households.

Although many single parents did meet the standard of success, results of both the parenting scale and the focus group support the need for review of the materials with the nontraditional family structure in mind.

Staff review of these results agreed that the curriculum focused too heavily on two-parent households but that many of the suggestions could easily be applied to single-parent households if minor adjustments were made. Staff believed that topic presentations and discussions could make a point to focus on single parents' and other parenting households' special needs for managing child behavior.

Recommendations and Commendations

The last element included in all evaluation reports is a section on recommendations and commendations. Recommendations, of course, should state what the program needs to do to improve its outcomes or reporting of its outcomes. This could mean training staff in program content, devising new record-keeping procedures, changing recruiting practices, and so forth.

What the program does well should also be part of the evaluation report. Focusing on the negative only harms stakeholder groups' perceptions of the program and prevents them from seeing the whole picture. Many programs have outcomes that meet standards consistently from year to year. This should be underscored for the reader. Good programs should duplicate what they do well and eliminate elements that prevent achieving standards of success. Providing a well-balanced picture of the program gives stakeholder groups insight into the goals and achievements of the program regardless of their association and experience with the program.

Example 1: Recommendations and Commendations

Given the results of this year's evaluation, the following recommendations are offered:

- Complete a literature review on single-parent needs and review curriculum to address their needs.
- Develop handouts that emphasize concepts and offer various strategies for managing a child's behavior.
- To eliminate overlap in the topics covered, solicit feedback from the participants at the end of each session regarding relevance of the materials covered.

The following commendations are offered:

- The program was successful in meeting the standard of success for more than 60% of participants.
- Participants identified the program practices of group discussion and handouts as helping them understand program concepts and encouraging them to apply these concepts.

Graphics

Graphics present pictures of the results and can be very useful in emphasizing points made in the text and or tables in the report. Bar graphs, line graphs, and pie charts help the reader visualize what results look like. Graphs emphasize differences and make it easier to compare data. In the report used as an example, a graph would fit well in the participants' section, providing a graphic representation of the percent of participants in each type of parenting household. Figures 3 and 4 are two examples of graphs that present the same results.

■ Executive Summaries

Executive summaries are brief statements of evaluation results. They provide an overview of the program and are designed to be read quickly. Executive summaries are written after a full report has been completed. Many details included in

Figure 3. Percent of Parenting Households

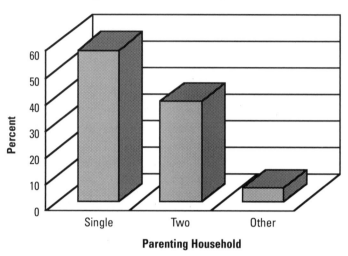

Figure 4. Percent of Parenting Households

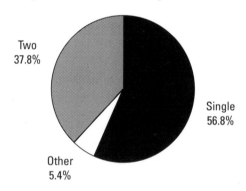

the full report are trimmed from the executive summary. An executive summary should also reference the full report for readers who wish further information.

Example 1: Executive Summary of Parenting Program Results
　　The goal of the Parenting Program is to help parents of children younger than six years of age gain an understanding of effective parenting and discipline practices. The program is conducted in 10 sessions and uses various techniques (lecture, discussion, homework, etc.) to achieve this goal.

To measure this gain the Parenting Practice Scale is used as a pre- and posttest measure. A gain of 20 or more points for 70% of the participants is considered the program's standard of success.

This year results of the 38 target-population participants indicated the following:

- More than 60% of the participants gained 20 or more points on the posttest. This is consistent with results of the past two program years.
- Almost 86% of the partnered (traditional) parents met the standard of success.
- Approximately 67% of the single parents met the standard of success.

Feedback from participants included:
- More participant discussion time.
- More homework handouts with new techniques discussed in the program.
- More emphasis on single-parent needs.
- Shortening the number of sessions from 10 to 8.

Staff reviewed the results and offered the following recommendations for program improvement in 1996–1997:
- Complete a literature review on single parents and review curriculum.
- Develop homework handouts.
- Obtain feedback session by session for topic relevance.

Staff also commented on the program's strengths.
- The program was successful in meeting its standard of success in 60% of participants.
- Current practice of group discussion and handouts helped participants understand concepts.

For more complete details of results, please refer to the complete report or contact [name of evaluator].

The executive summary provides an efficient and concise overview of the program's success. It does not, however, give the complete picture. Unfortunately, many administrative decisions are made on executive summaries alone. Therefore, extreme care must be taken regarding the information presented in an executive summary as well as in how this information is presented. A presentation of the results with the full report attached to the executive summary can help ensure that the stakeholder group will obtain a complete picture of the program.

■ Summary

This chapter presented an example of an evaluation report and an executive summary. The report ties together prior years' information, current results, and future activities of the program.

Program evaluation reports should be products of the staff (or selected staff). Although an evaluator manages the information and writes the report, staff should provide input into reasons for the results and make recommendations for program improvement.

Executive summaries provide a useful overview of results but should be accompanied by the full report and, when it is possible, a presentation of the results. This is done to give stakeholders a complete picture of a program's success.

To Do

1. Outline report.
2. Draft results and send to staff for review.
3. Identify results that need text, tables, and graphs.
4. Formulate recommendations and commendations.
5. Finalize report and draft executive summary.
6. Review executive summary.
7. Prepare report for distribution to stakeholder groups.
8. Prepare presentation.
